For International Students Applying to University in the USA

THE UNIVERSITY BOUND ORGANIZER

D1552345

The Ultimate Guide to Successful Applications to American Universities

ANNA COSTARAS & GAIL LISS

Foreword by Edward B. Fiske, author of Fiske Guide to College

Copyright © 2019 Anna Costaras and Gail Liss.
Published by Mango Publishing Group, a division of Mango Media Inc.

Cover Design: Roberto Nuñez
Layout Design: Elina Diaz

Mango is an active supporter of authors' rights to free speech and artistic expression in their books. The purpose of copyright is to encourage authors to produce exceptional works that enrich our culture and our open society.

Uploading or distributing photos, scans or any content from this book without prior permission is theft of the authors' intellectual property. Please honor the authors' work as you would your own. Thank you in advance for respecting our authors' rights.

For permission requests, please contact the publisher at:

Mango Publishing Group
2850 Douglas Road, 2nd Floor
Suite 201
Coral Gables, FL 33134 USA
info@mango.bz

For special orders, quantity sales, course adoptions and corporate sales, please email the publisher at sales@mango.bz. For trade and wholesale sales, please contact Ingram Publisher Services at customer.service@ingramcontent.com or +1.800.509.4887.

The University Bound Organizer: The Ultimate Guide to Successful Applications to American Universities

Library of Congress Cataloging
ISBN: (print)978-1-64250-108-7, (ebook) 978-1-64250-109-4
Library of Congress Control Number: 2019938540
BISAC category code : EDU015000 EDUCATION/Higher

Printed in the United States of America

Emmy, Jessica and Alix
and
James, Christopher and Michael

Thank you for leading us down this unexpected path.

TABLE OF CONTENTS

FOREWORD   *07*

INTRODUCTION   *09*

CHAPTER 1 | GETTING STARTED: FACT FINDING   *11*

    Student's Personal Information   14

    Family Education Information   16

    Secondary School Information   17

CHAPTER 2 | A SNAPSHOT OF YOUR SECONDARY SCHOOL YEARS: WHO ARE YOU?   *19*

    Clubs & Extracurricular Activities   27

    Sports   31

    Community Service   35

    Awards   39

    Competitions   40

    Work Experience   44

    Summer Experiences   45

    Letters of Recommendation   49

CHAPTER 3 | TESTING A TO Z: TRACK YOUR SCORES   *51*

    Standardized Test Schedule   58

    Test Prep Resources   59

    Standardized Test Scores   60

CHAPTER 4 | RESEARCHING SCHOOLS: GETTING ACQUAINTED   65

School Search   79

Meetings and Interviews   104

Correspondence Journal   116

CHAPTER 5 | DEFINE YOUR CHOICES: YOU'RE READY TO APPLY!   127

Application Checklist   138

CHAPTER 6 | PAYING THE BILLS: FINDING THE FUNDS   141

Financial Aid Worksheet   148

Scholarship Log   150

CHAPTER 7 | THE HOME STRETCH: YOU'RE ALMOST DONE!   153

Am I In?   161

Should I / Shouldn't I?   162

CHAPTER 8 | THE INTERVIEWS   165

Conversations With College Admissions Officers   165

Conversations With Secondary School Professionals   191

RESOURCES   201
ACKNOWLEDGMENTS   203
ABOUT THE AUTHORS   205

FOREWORD

There are more than 2,200 four-year colleges in the United States, and trying to figure out which ones are likely to be good matches for *you* can seem like a daunting task. It's easy to sympathize with the applicant to Haverford College some years ago, who was particularly stressed out at the end of his on-campus interview. On his way back to the waiting room he had to pass through several doors, but his emotional state was such that he failed to notice where he was and opened one more door—which took him into a closet. He was so embarrassed that he remained in the closet for several minutes before reappearing to face a room full of staring faces.

It doesn't have to be that way. As author of the *Fiske Guide to Colleges* and numerous other books on college admissions, I've had the pleasure of working with thousands of college-bound high school students and their parents both in person and through my writing. People are not born brain-wired knowing how to navigate the byzantine admissions process that American colleges and universities have, in their wisdom, imposed on their aspiring students, so a bit of anxiety—or at least mild bewilderment—is probably a sign that you are in touch with reality.

Not surprisingly, the most common question that I have gotten over the years from students staring at all those options is: "Where do I start?" The implicit subtext is: "How do I begin to make sense of the process?" My usual (and admittedly self-serving) suggestion is to thumb through the 300+ narrative descriptions in the *Fiske Guide* and find one or two schools that seem like a good match. Then look at the schools with which these schools have substantial overlapping applicant pools and maybe look at overlaps of the overlaps. This process should produce a list of 15 or 20 target schools to get you off and running.

Once you have identified some target schools, the challenge is to figure out how to deal with all the elements that go into the application process: campus visits, test-taking, financial aid forms, letters of reference, and so forth. That, of course, is where *The College Bound Organizer* comes to your rescue in at least two ways. First, it gives you a "one-stop shopping" way to keep track of the hundreds of details that go into applying to multiple colleges. No more ruffling through piles of papers to figure out when—or even whether!—you have scheduled an appointment with the admissions folks at Old Siwash. Second, it represents a checklist—with deadlines—that lays out the various steps that you need to be taking. With *The College Bound Organizer* at your side, you can rest assured that you will not wake up on December 31 and suddenly realize that you forgot to ask your English teacher for a recommendation that is due two days later.

Applying to college should be a positive experience. Colleges are interesting places, with lots of bright people doing innovative things, and the application process is really the beginning of your college education. It's the time when you begin to think seriously about your goals and academic interests. The mechanics of the process are important and need to be taken seriously. But it's also important to keep your mind on the big picture: which colleges are best suited to help you to grow academically, socially, spiritually, and in every other way? Using *The College Bound Organizer* is one way to help you stay focused on what is really important.

Edward B. Fiske
Author of Fiske Guide to Colleges

INTRODUCTION

Whether you're just beginning to think about your future plans or are committed to attending university in the United States, we're here to help you find your way. Applying to university (most commonly referred to as *college*) in the USA as an international applicant is complicated and can seem like an overwhelming process. Don't underestimate the time required to complete your search and application process. Together, we are going to break it down into a series of many small, manageable tasks. With a well-thought-out plan and a good organizing system, you will have all the tools you'll need to put together an outstanding application and get the best admissions results possible.

The college application process is daunting for both students and their parents. It's a maze of deadlines, test prep, testing, college fairs, campus tours, applications, curriculum vitae (CV), essays, interviews and financial aid forms. As an international applicant, you may also be required to submit your academic transcript to a credential evaluator. It goes without saying that you will be required to do all this while continuing to stay focused on academics, athletics, extracurricular commitments, jobs, family responsibilities and all the interests, obligations, and activities that fill your day. Your life is now filled with college chaos.

Here's your challenge: to successfully apply to university. This will require you to define yourself by understanding who you are, identifying your goals, finding schools that fit your profile, staying on task to meet deadlines, and correctly submitting all your application components in a well-executed manner. Here's your solution: *The University Bound Organizer.* Our method will help keep you focused and on task, allowing you to organize and manage the massive amount of information that you will be responsible for creating, requesting, and submitting while meeting all the different due dates for your applications. Our road map will steer you through the stressful university application process and get you to the school that's a good fit for you. To keep you in touch with what today's educators are thinking, a select group of admissions professionals were consulted and are quoted throughout the book.

Planning to attend university in the USA is exciting! There is much to look forward to: being independent, challenging yourself, acquiring new skills, having new experiences, meeting different people, exploring a variety of interests, making friends, and of course, learning so many new things. You'll have a tremendous number of decisions to make, from course selection, to focus of study, to career options to pursue. But first, you have to get there.

Let's get started!

Anna and Gail

CHAPTER 1

GETTING STARTED: FACT FINDING

When applying to university you will be required to provide facts about yourself, your family, and your school, repeatedly. You'll be asked for this information countless times when registering for tests, completing your applications, and applying for financial aid and scholarships. Easy access to this information will help you avoid endless aggravation. Having this information organized in one place will also minimize the chance that you'll make mistakes on your applications.

Begin with the **Student's Personal Information** worksheet provided in this chapter. Start by setting up an email account to use exclusively for your school search and application process, then record this on the worksheet. Universities will be communicating with you via email and having a separate account makes it less likely that you'll miss an important notice in your inbox. The schools you apply to will send many important announcements to help you complete your applications. Get into the habit of checking your email at least once a day.

If your email address reflects some funny nickname or private joke you have with your friends, get a new one! Set up an address that is appropriate and easy to read. This is part of the identity you present to admissions officers.

> **"It's a fine idea to have an email address that's just for college applications, but if you do, check that email. I see hundreds of high school seniors missing opportunities because they're not in the regular email habit."**
>
> **—JONATHAN BURDICK, Dean of Admissions and Financial Aid, University of Rochester**

> **"Think about what your email address may or may not say about you."**
>
> **—ALISON ALMASIAN, Director of Admissions, St. Lawrence University**

Next on the **Student's Personal Information** worksheet, list your user names and passwords once you register for standardized tests including SAT, ACT, and /or TOEFL or IELTS. College Board administers the SAT and SAT Subject Test, ACT administers the ACT exam, ETS administers TOEFL and IELTS administers the IELTS exam. To learn more about these tests refer to Chapter 3.

Most students apply to university by using the Common Application and/or individual school applications. The Common App is a single, uniform application accepted by approximately 800 colleges and universities. The Common App allows you to create one application which you can submit to multiple participating schools, either online or by mail. Create an account for the Common App and record your username and password on the same worksheet. In addition, you will create accounts for each school to which you apply. Jot down these usernames and passwords on the worksheet as well.

> **"One way to stay organized is to keep a list of the schools you applied to next to your computer with each school's username and password. The username and password always vary based on school,**

> **and it is best to be able to easily access this information. Students often become frustrated when they forget this information, and that only delays this process."**
>
> **—REBECCA GOTTESMAN, Assistant Principal, Locust Valley High School, Locust Valley, New York**

Students applying for financial aid and merit scholarships may be required to complete the financial aid form called the CSS/Financial Aid PROFILE, a financial aid form required by many schools. Record the user name, password, and PIN you create for this account on the worksheet.

You'll need to gather information from your family members about their education history to complete your applications. Store all of the information and facts about your parents and your siblings on the **Family Education Information** worksheet.

Details about your education thus far should be noted on the **Secondary School Information** worksheet. You'll need to know your school's international SAT and ACT codes, found on the testing websites, in order to register for your standardized tests. Use this worksheet to write down your secondary school contact information, as it will be required when you complete the Common App. This same information is also needed for colleges and universities that only accept their own applications. Spare yourself repeated searches by looking all this up once and recording it in the designated space.

Student's Personal Information

Email _____

SAT

User Name _____ Password _____

ACT

User Name _____ Password _____

IELTS

User Name _____ Password _____

TOEFL

User Name _____ Password _____

COMMON APPLICATION

User Name _____ Password _____

CSS/PROFILE

User Name _____ Password _____

Student's Personal Information

School Name: _____
User Name: _____
Password: _____
Student ID #: _____

School Name: _____
User Name: _____
Password: _____
Student ID #: _____

School Name: _____
User Name: _____
Password: _____
Student ID #: _____

School Name: _____
User Name: _____
Password: _____
Student ID #: _____

School Name: _____
User Name: _____
Password: _____
Student ID #: _____

School Name: _____
User Name: _____
Password: _____
Student ID #: _____

School Name: _____
User Name: _____
Password: _____
Student ID #: _____

School Name: _____
User Name: _____
Password: _____
Student ID #: _____

School Name: _____
User Name: _____
Password: _____
Student ID #: _____

School Name: _____
User Name: _____
Password: _____
Student ID #: _____

School Name: _____
User Name: _____
Password: _____
Student ID #: _____

School Name: _____
User Name: _____
Password: _____
Student ID #: _____

Family Education Information

MOTHER

Undergraduate School
Degree/Date of Graduation
Graduate School
Degree/Date of Graduation
Graduate School
Degree/Date of Graduation

FATHER

Undergraduate School
Degree/Date of Graduation
Graduate School
Degree/Date of Graduation
Graduate School
Degree/Date of Graduation

SIBLING

Undergraduate School
Degree/Date of Graduation

SIBLING

Undergraduate School
Degree/Date of Graduation

SIBLING

Undergraduate School
Degree/Date of Graduation

Secondary School Information

School Name _____

Address _____

_____

SAT Code _____

ACT Code _____

School Counselor Name _____

Telephone _____

Email _____

Additional Contact Name _____

Telephone _____

Email _____

Additional Contact Name _____

Telephone _____

Email _____

CHAPTER 2

A SNAPSHOT OF YOUR SECONDARY SCHOOL YEARS: WHO ARE YOU?

Admissions reps work very hard to put together each year's incoming class. The goal of the admissions office is to build a qualified, well-rounded first year class. Your goal is to find a university that meets your needs and matches your profile. Keep in mind that the terms "college" and "university" are used interchangeably in the USA in everyday speech. An institution of higher learning is most often referred to as a college. Colleges and universities generally look at applicants from several angles to determine whether they're a good fit. Your academic performance and test scores are the starting point for admissions, but there's so much more that will be considered. American universities evaluate students holistically. In addition to your grades, admissions reps are also interested in your extracurricular activities including athletics, community service, clubs, competitions, work, and summer experiences. Think about the person you would like admissions officers to get to know. Reveal your identity through extracurricular interests and involvement, your essays, the words of your recommenders and your social media presence.

> **"Both colleges and students have a duty to communicate who they are as effectively as possible to ensure the best possible matches."**
>
> **—ALISON ALMASIAN, Director of Admissions,
>   St. Lawrence University**

ACADEMICS

Your academic record is the foundation of your application. Universities view the grades you've achieved as the best predictor of your future academic success. The level of difficulty of the classes you've taken and your grades are the primary yardstick by which you will be evaluated. You can find a university's core academic requirements listed on its website. Beyond meeting the requirements, admissions reps want to see what academic interests you've pursued. Highly competitive schools are looking for students who have taken the most rigorous courses offered at their secondary school. Consult your counselor to plan the curriculum most suited to you. But, remember the college process in the USA is not only about academics.

EXTRACURRICULARS

Each student brings his or her own identity to the campus. You can show admissions representatives who you are through your extracurricular activities, including athletics, community service, work experience, and summer activities. Universities look at the breadth and depth to which you have explored your interests. Your choices reflect your values and your personality. Your extracurricular involvement not only tells colleges and universities what you've done throughout secondary school, but also conveys how you may contribute to their community as a prospective member. Everyone has different interests and one interest is not necessarily better than another. What's important is why and how you chose to become involved, and what it means to you. Don't paint a picture of who you think Admissions is looking for. Demonstrate, with authenticity, the real you. You'll have the opportunity to share your personal profile with Admissions on your applications, either in the Activities section of the Common App, in an individual school application, or if requested, in an uploaded CV. Whether you've just started secondary school or are an upper-level student, explore school clubs and organizations, volunteer opportunities and hobbies in order to identify extracurriculars you would enjoy pursuing. Once you've found what interests you, get involved. What counts is the extent of your commitment, not the length of your activities list. Your engagement outside the classroom speaks to who you are and may be what differentiates you from your peers. Balancing schoolwork and commitments outside the classroom also demonstrates your time management skills.

> **"Students should consider highlighting the things into which they have poured the most time and effort, finding the things that have meant the most to them and the things in which they have made the greatest impact. Students need to understand that college admissions officers are trying to get a sense of the individual by evaluating how that individual has spent his or her time."**
>
> —PAUL W. HORGAN, Director of College Counseling, Cape Henry Collegiate School, Virginia Beach, Virginia

> **"Representing all that you do beyond academics with authenticity is very important."**
>
> —DARRYL W. JONES, Senior Associate Director of Admissions, Gettysburg College

This chapter provides seven *Who Are You?* worksheets to help you easily fill in the activities sections of your applications. Worksheets are provided for four years of secondary school. These worksheets will also help you to create a CV to submit either as a supplement to the Common App or to individual school applications. Your CV can also be used when you apply for internships and jobs. Identify the worksheets that apply to you and gather the information necessary to compile a complete and accurate profile of your secondary school years. Although you'll find some of the categories overlap, list your activities on the worksheet you think fits best. Think about all the things you were involved with outside the classroom and list your activities in order of importance to you. You don't need to include everything you've been involved in during secondary school, but instead list the things you feel help define who you are. If it's hard to remember everything you've done, ask your family to help you put together your list.

✓ **Clubs & Extracurricular Activities** worksheet: include activities such as academic and social clubs, debate club, school newspaper, yearbook, music, theatre/drama, culture and art, both in and outside of school. Any hobbies you spend a considerable amount of time on are also relevant. Universities are particularly interested in any leadership positions you've held, so don't forget to include your titles and responsibilities.

✓ **Sports** worksheet: list all your teams, tournaments, and awards for athletic involvement in school-sponsored and independently run leagues. Again, emphasize any leadership roles.

✓ **Community Service** worksheet: note your service involvement, both school-sponsored and independent. Include volunteering, tutoring and fundraising activities. What's important here is your level of involvement and genuine commitment, so there's no need to include your one visit to the local food bank.

✓ **Awards** worksheet: explain all the academic achievements and non-academic distinctions you've earned throughout your secondary school years. Include significant commitment to programs such as science research or athletics. Awards include anything from a math fair placement to a hip-hop dance trophy.

Don't stress!

These worksheets are here to help you sort through and organize your secondary school experiences.

✓ **Competitions** worksheet: describe any contests in which you participated or are currently involved. These may include, but are not limited to, science, math or engineering events, writing submissions, art exhibitions and debates.

✓ **Work Experience** worksheet: demonstrate your work ethic by noting any paid and unpaid jobs and internships you have had. There are all types of jobs, including caring for your younger siblings.

✓ **Summer Experiences** worksheet: note any summer activities including work, travel, academic courses or programs, athletics and community outreach. How you spend your summer breaks shows Admissions what you choose to do with your free time.

RECOMMENDATIONS

Recommendations are an important component of your application because they allow colleges and universities to see beyond your grades and test scores. A good recommendation letter is one that offers admissions reps a chance to get to know you. Most colleges require a recommendation from your counselor and a letter from one or two of your teachers.

Letters from your school counselor will help admissions officers understand more about your school, its programs, curriculum, and requirements, and the student body. These letters help to define your standing within your school community and your achievements relative to those of your peers. Teachers' letters provide insight into your learning style and your academic development, which speaks to your potential for engagement and achievement in a college classroom. You may consider including an additional letter if you've made a significant commitment to a program (such as fine arts or athletics) or if there's someone outside the classroom who can share a valuable perspective. Here are some helpful tips to consider when requesting your recommendations:

> If you attend a large school and don't know your counselor, set up a meeting to get acquainted. If you have any special circumstances (health, family, finances) that you'd like explained in the letter, let your counselor know at this time. Talk to your counselor about your hopes and dreams for college and provide as much background information as possible for a strong letter in support of your applications.

> Offer your recommenders a copy of your CV to give them a more complete picture of who you are and to help them write an effective letter.

> Make your request for recommendations in person. The ideal time to ask is in the spring prior to your final year of secondary school. Make sure to confirm with your recommenders in the fall of your final year. If you're currently in the last year of secondary school and have not yet made this request, ask now. Many teachers receive more requests than they can fulfill, so asking in advance allows them to put you on their list.

> Most colleges and universities require that letters be written by instructors you had in your last two years of secondary school.

If possible, ask primary subject teachers. Also, remember, a recommendation will be more valuable if written by a teacher who knows you well and likes you.

➤ Provide your teachers with information that will help them write a letter that speaks to your learning style, aptitude, potential and character. Give them an outline of the highlights of your time spent in their classroom, your favorite assignments, and samples of your work. Let them know what you enjoy(ed) most about their class. Share anything you've done outside the classroom that is relevant to their subject matter. Help them write a letter that ties together all your related experiences.

➤ If your school participates in an online program, your writers will submit their recommendations electronically. If by chance your school still mails in the forms, provide each writer with a recommendation form for each college along with a stamped, addressed envelope. Give each recommender a list of your schools and the application deadlines.

➤ Use the **Letters of Recommendation** worksheet to jot down the date you give your teachers the forms. Check on the schools' online portals or call the admissions offices as the process progresses to confirm receipt of the letters.

SOCIAL MEDIA

Your social media profile is another way to define yourself to Admissions. Much has been said about social media and its impact on college admissions. Your online presence is a very important consideration. Use social media to project an image you are proud of. Make sure you aren't represented in a way you would be uncomfortable sharing with your admissions reps or interviewers. Before you begin the college process, consider doing the following:

> Use social media to connect with college reps and demonstrate your interest in their school.

> Make sure your photos convey the image you want to project, highlighting activities that are important to you and reflect your interests.

> Make sure to delete any photos that are inappropriate.

> Remove yourself from any groups that you don't want to be defined by.

> Don't write anything that you wouldn't want an admissions rep to read.

> Use social media sites to highlight positive things about yourself.

Clubs/ Extracurricular Activities

ACADEMIC YEAR _____

Name:	Dates:
Description:	
Position:	

Name:	Dates:
Description:	
Position:	

Name:	Dates:
Description:	
Position:	

Name:	Dates:
Description:	
Position:	

Name:	Dates:
Description:	
Position:	

Clubs/ Extracurricular Activities

ACADEMIC YEAR _____

Name:	Dates:
Description:	
Position:	

Name:	Dates:
Description:	
Position:	

Name:	Dates:
Description:	
Position:	

Name:	Dates:
Description:	
Position:	

Name:	Dates:
Description:	
Position:	

Clubs/ Extracurricular Activities

ACADEMIC YEAR _____

Name:	Dates:
Description:	
Position:	

Name:	Dates:
Description:	
Position:	

Name:	Dates:
Description:	
Position:	

Name:	Dates:
Description:	
Position:	

Name:	Dates:
Description:	
Position:	

Clubs/ Extracurricular Activities

ACADEMIC YEAR _____

Name:	Dates:
Description:	
Position:	

Name:	Dates:
Description:	
Position:	

Name:	Dates:
Description:	
Position:	

Name:	Dates:
Description:	
Position:	

Name:	Dates:
Description:	
Position:	

Sports

ACADEMIC YEAR _____

SPORT 1:	
Team 1:	Position:
Team 2:	Position:
Team 3:	Position:

SPORT 2:	
Team 1:	Position:
Team 2:	Position:
Team 3:	Position:

SPORT 3:	
TEAM 1:	Position:
TEAM 2:	Position:
TEAM 3:	Position:

Sports

ACADEMIC YEAR _____

SPORT 1:	
Team 1:	Position:
Team 2:	Position:
Team 3:	Position:

SPORT 2:	
Team 1:	Position:
Team 2:	Position:
Team 3:	Position:

SPORT 3:	
Team 1:	Position:
Team 2:	Position:
Team 3:	Position:

Sports

ACADEMIC YEAR _____

SPORT 1:	
Team 1:	Position:
Team 2:	Position:
Team 3:	Position:

SPORT 2:	
Team 1:	Position:
Team 2:	Position:
Team 3:	Position:

SPORT 3:	
Team 1:	Position:
Team 2:	Position:
Team 3:	Position:

Sports

ACADEMIC YEAR _____

SPORT 1:	
Team 1:	Position:
Team 2:	Position:
Team 3:	Position:

SPORT 2:	
Team 1:	Position:
Team 2:	Position:
Team 3:	Position:

SPORT 3:	
Team 1:	Position:
Team 2:	Position:
Team 3:	Position:

Community Service

ACADEMIC YEAR _____

Name of Organization:
Description of Role:
Dates:

Name of Organization:
Description of Role:
Dates:

Name of Organization:
Description of Role:
Dates:

Name of Organization:
Description of Role:
Dates:

Name of Organization:
Description of Role:
Dates:

Community Service

ACADEMIC YEAR _____

Name of Organization:
Description of Role:
Dates:

Name of Organization:
Description of Role:
Dates:

Name of Organization:
Description of Role:
Dates:

Name of Organization:
Description of Role:
Dates:

Name of Organization:
Description of Role:
Dates:

Community Service

ACADEMIC YEAR _____

Name of Organization:
Description of Role:
Dates:

Name of Organization:
Description of Role:
Dates:

Name of Organization:
Description of Role:
Dates:

Name of Organization:
Description of Role:
Dates:

Name of Organization:
Description of Role:
Dates:

Community Service

ACADEMIC YEAR _____

Name of Organization:
Description of Role:
Dates:

Name of Organization:
Description of Role:
Dates:

Name of Organization:
Description of Role:
Dates:

Name of Organization:
Description of Role:
Dates:

Name of Organization:
Description of Role:
Dates:

Awards

ACADEMIC YEAR _____

NAME OF AWARD	DATE

ACADEMIC YEAR _____

NAME OF AWARD	DATE

ACADEMIC YEAR _____

NAME OF AWARD	DATE

ACADEMIC YEAR _____

NAME OF AWARD	DATE

Competitions

ACADEMIC YEAR _____

Competition:
Project:
Date:
Outcome:

Competition:
Project:
Date:
Outcome:

Competition:
Project:
Date:
Outcome:

Competition:
Project:
Date:
Outcome:

Competition:
Project:
Date:
Outcome:

Competitions

ACADEMIC YEAR _____

Competition:
Project:
Date:
Outcome:

Competition:
Project:
Date:
Outcome:

Competition:
Project:
Date:
Outcome:

Competition:
Project:
Date:
Outcome:

Competition:
Project:
Date:
Outcome:

Competitions

ACADEMIC YEAR _____

Competition:
Project:
Date:
Outcome:

Competition:
Project:
Date:
Outcome:

Competition:
Project:
Date:
Outcome:

Competition:
Project:
Date:
Outcome:

Competition:
Project:
Date:
Outcome:

Competitions

ACADEMIC YEAR _____

Competition:
Project:
Date:
Outcome:

Competition:
Project:
Date:
Outcome:

Competition:
Project:
Date:
Outcome:

Competition:
Project:
Date:
Outcome:

Competition:
Project:
Date:
Outcome:

Work Experience

ACADEMIC YEAR _____

Employer:

Job Description:

Dates:

ACADEMIC YEAR _____

Employer:

Job Description:

Dates:

ACADEMIC YEAR _____

Employer:

Job Description:

Dates:

ACADEMIC YEAR _____

Employer:

Job Description:

Dates:

Summer Experiences

ACADEMIC YEAR _____

Dates:

Description:

Dates:

Description:

Dates:

Description:

Dates:

Description:

Dates:

Description:

Summer Experiences

ACADEMIC YEAR _____

Dates:
Description:

Dates:
Description:

Dates:
Description:

Dates:
Description:

Dates:
Description:

Summary Experiences

ACADEMIC YEAR _____

Dates:
Description:

Dates:
Description:

Dates:
Description:

Dates:
Description:

Dates:
Description:

Summer Experiences

ACADEMIC YEAR _____

Dates:

Description:

Dates:

Description:

Dates:

Description:

Dates:

Description:

Dates:

Description:

Letters of Recommendation

Name:
Email:
Telephone:
Date Requested:

Name:
Email:
Telephone:
Date Requested:

Name:
Email:
Telephone:
Date Requested:

Name:
Email:
Telephone:
Date Requested:

CHAPTER 3

TESTING A TO Z: TRACK YOUR SCORES

Now is the time to become familiar with the alphabet soup of standardized tests: PSAT, ACT, SAT, SAT Subject Tests (SAT IIs), TOEFL, and IELTS. There is no denying standardized testing is an important part of the university application process. Test scores are among the many criteria used to evaluate your candidacy. Once you are accepted, a college or university may also use your scores to award scholarships, determine placement in classes, and offer admission to special programs.

TESTS

PSAT: The PSAT is a "practice" test for the SAT, given every October. Consult with your school counselor to determine whether and in which year of secondary school to sit for this exam. In December, College Board will send your score reports to your secondary school. Consult the College Board website for a detailed explanation on how the test is scored and then review your scores to decide what you need to work on before you take the SAT.

SAT: The SAT is a multiple choice standardized test widely used for college admissions in the USA. The two main sections of the SAT are Evidence-Based Reading & Writing and Math. The total score is a combination of these sections, each being scored out of 800. The highest composite score is 800 plus 800, or 1600.

The essay in the SAT is optional and will not be factored into the overall SAT score. The essay is scored on three measures: Reading, Analysis, and Writing. Each component is scored on a scale of 2 to 8 and results appear on a separate score report. Consult with your counselor to decide whether to sign up for the essay component.

SAT SUBJECT TESTS: SAT Subject Tests (SAT IIs) are one hour multiple choice standardized tests given in 20 individual subjects. Each exam is scored on a scale from 200-800, just like the individual sections of the SAT. A student may take up to three SAT Subject Tests on any given date at a flat rate, but cannot take both the SAT and Subject Tests on the same day. Some selective colleges, either recommend or require scores from at least two SAT Subject Tests. Check individual school websites for specific details.

ACT: The ACT is another standardized test used for college admissions in the United States and is an alternative to the SAT. The ACT is a multiple choice exam which tests students in four areas: English, math, reading and science with an optional writing section. Each subject is given a scaled score between 1 and 36. Those scores are then averaged into a composite score, also ranging between 1 and 36. Because the ACT writing section is optional, that score will not be factored into the overall composite score.

PLANNING

Don't let all the talk about upcoming test options overwhelm you. Instead, map out a plan to make sure you take the necessary tests on the optimal dates and have enough time to prepare. The following steps will help you develop your best course of action:

> ➢ Find out which tests are required. As you start to think about schools that interest you, look through their websites for information on testing. Most schools allow you to submit either the ACT or SAT. Requirements for SAT IIs vary from school to

school. While there are schools that require one, two or even three tests, some ask for none at all.

➢ Determine which test is best for you. Take online ACT and SAT practice tests in order to compare your scores. Get input from your counselor and your parents to help you decide.

➢ If you've taken the PSAT, review your results, which offer valuable feedback, if you've decided to take the SAT. Identify your strengths and weaknesses and focus your efforts on the sections you would like to improve.

➢ Arrange for special testing accommodations, if necessary. Talk to your guidance counselor for information or contact ACT and/or College Board for details.

➢ Consider test-optional schools. Hundreds of colleges and universities do not require test scores as a part of their application process, but instead offer a more holistic admissions approach.

➢ Plan your testing schedule. Look at ACT and SAT test dates for the entire school year, choose dates that allow you enough time to prepare and take as many practice tests as you can.

➢ Confirm registration deadlines and sign up as soon as possible to ensure your spot at the location of your choice. Review the test schedule to best plan as not all tests are offered on every test date.

➢ Determine the optimal time to schedule SAT II exams. SAT II scores demonstrate your proficiency in a specific subject, so work closely with your counselor and teachers to develop a strategy. For example, it may be best to take a particular subject test immediately after you've completed the corresponding course on the same subject, when the material is freshest in your mind.

- ➢ Avoid scheduling conflicts. Make sure your family is aware of your testing schedule to confirm your availability and to assure you'll have a ride to the test, if needed.

- ➢ Register for your tests. Sign up online with College Board (for the SAT and SAT IIs), and with ACT for the ACT exam. If applicable, to demonstrate English proficiency, register with ETS for the TOEFL exam or with the IELTS for the IELTS exam.

- ➢ Have a current photo on hand when you sign up for your tests. ACT and College Board registrations both require you to submit a photograph of yourself for security purposes.

- ➢ Get organized. As you determine the tests you need to take, use the **Standardized Test Schedule** provided in this chapter to keep track of the test dates, registration deadlines and locations you've registered for.

- ➢ Print your admission ticket once your registration is complete. For safe keeping, file your ticket in a folder which you should label **General**.

The night before the SAT, as John S. frantically searched for his registration ticket, he realized he had never hit the "submit" button. After a sleepless night, he and his mother rushed to the test center and, in a frenzy, completed the necessary forms to secure a spot on the standby list.

On that note, remember to bring a calculator, sharpened number 2 pencils and the required ID. Otherwise, it will be a long ride home. You may also want a water bottle, a snack, extra calculator batteries, a watch, and maybe even a sweatshirt.

> **"With multiple deadlines and tasks to keep on top of, it's easy for something to fall through the cracks."**
>
> **—LAURA A. BRUNO, Assistant Vice Chancellor for Enrollment Strategy and Management, The City University of New York**

Over 800 colleges and universities have adopted a test-optional policy. Check FairTest's website for a list of test optional schools. These schools do not require standardized test scores to make admissions decisions because they believe test scores are not necessarily representative of a student's abilities or academic potential. While test scores are not required, you can still choose to submit them to be reviewed as part of your application if you are happy with your scores and feel they accurately reflect your ability. Ask your counselor for advice if you're thinking of going the test-optional route.

In lieu of standardized test scores, test-optional schools may instead ask students to submit other materials including, writing samples, portfolios, and International Baccalaureate (IB) scores. Greater emphasis may be placed on other components of the application, including your secondary school transcript, interviews with admissions reps and graded assignments from your last two years of secondary school. If the test-optional path is for you, locate schoolwork you're proud of and save it in your **General** folder.

Make sure to check individual school requirements for exceptions. International applicants, students who are homeschooled and those who attend schools that do not use a grading system may be required to submit standardized test scores.

PREPARING

The majority of students do opt to take either the ACT or SAT. Achieving the best possible scores will require you to develop your own test-taking strategy.

Match your prep with your learning style and your budget. You can opt to prepare on your own, in a group or with a tutor. Helpful resources include: prep books, online courses, group prep programs and private tutors. Ask your counselor, parents and people you know who have studied in the USA for recommendations when deciding on a prep method. Part of preparing is learning how to pace yourself, managing your timing and understanding how the tests are scored. It's essential to become familiar with the tests by taking as many practice exams as possible. Take advantage of the free resources listed below:

For the SAT and SAT Subject Tests:

1. College Board has both online and printed versions of official practice tests.

2. College Board has an app that features a new practice question daily to build your familiarity with the SAT.

3. College Board offers free sample practice questions in math, reading and writing for the SAT on their website.

4. Many test prep companies offer free practice tests, both online and at their test centers.

For the ACT:

1. A study guide and mobile app which include practice tests with scoring keys and test taking strategies are available from ACT.

2. ACT's website has practice questions in English, math, reading, science, and writing.

3. Sign up to receive an email from ACT with weekly questions.

4. Free online and on-site practice tests are available from a variety of test companies.

Keep track of all your test support usernames and passwords on the **Test Prep Resources** worksheet in this chapter.

Once you have your results, record all test dates and your corresponding scores on the **Standardized Test Scores** worksheet on page 58. This worksheet will help you list your test scores in an organized and easily accessible format. From this list, you will select your top scores to send to each school. When you receive your official standardized test score reports, file them in your **General** folder, as you may need to refer to them again.

Make sure to pay attention to college application deadlines to submit your scores on time. You can opt to take advantage of the limited free score reports that ACT and College Board offer when you register for your tests. In addition, at a later date, you can request and pay to submit additional scores by phone or online.

Standardardized Test Schedule

Test Date	Test	Location

Test Prep Resources

Website:
User Name:
Password:

Website:
User Name:
Password:

Website:
User Name:
Password:

Website:
User Name:
Password:

Website:
User Name:
Password:

Website:
User Name:
Password:

Website:
User Name:
Password:

Website:
User Name:
Password:

Standardized Test Scores

SAT

DATE	READING & WRITING	MATH	ESSAY (OPTIONAL)	OVERALL

SAT SUBJECT TESTS

SUBJECT:	
Date:	Score:
Date:	Score:

SUBJECT:	
Date:	Score:
Date:	Score:

SUBJECT:	
Date:	Score:
Date:	Score:

SUBJECT:	
Date:	Score:
Date:	Score:

ACT

DATE	ENGLISH	MATH	READING	SCIENCE	WRITING	COMPOSITE

TOEFL

DATE	READING	LISTENING	SPEAKING	WRITING	TOTAL

IELTS

DATE	READING	LISTENING	SPEAKING	WRITING	TOTAL

INTERNATIONAL BACCALAUREATE EXAMS

DATE	SUBJECT	SCORE

CHAPTER 4

RESEARCHING SCHOOLS: GETTING ACQUAINTED

Is there one perfect university for you? Perhaps. Most likely, though, there are many schools that could be a great fit. A "great fit" college should match your interests, abilities, and needs. The right school for you will have an environment you're comfortable with and programs to help you meet your long-term goals. Take into consideration academic programs and rigor, cost, geographic location, student body, clubs and activities, and your chance of admission. Each school has its unique personality. Whether visiting online, on campus or meeting with a school rep or alum, you'll sense the distinct characteristics that differentiate one school from another.

> **"I would like to say that students should always look for the right fit college and not be influenced only by the big name or the rank. Further, both applicants and admissions officers are partners in this endeavor and we have the same goal: students success."**
>
> **—Musa Khalidi, Executive Director International Admissions, St. Lawrence University**

There are over 4,000 colleges and universities to choose from in the USA. When you are doing your research, know the real differences. Universities are typically large institutions that offer both undergraduate and graduate programs and can be public or private. Often, universities are comprised of multiple colleges. College, as we said earlier, typically refers to institutions of higher learning that may be smaller and mainly focus on undergraduate education. Both colleges and universities are degree granting institutions.

> **"If you conduct your proper research to find out the academic profiles and requirements of the colleges you are interested in, heed the advice of your school counselors, and take the time to visit the colleges that you are considering, you will most likely find that after the application and admissions process is complete, you will be happy with the results. If you are honest with yourself and honest with the process, you will most likely find out that you end up at the college where you belong!"**
>
> **—KEVIN O'SULLIVAN, Director of Undergraduate Admissions, Manhattanville College**

With thousands of two- and four-year colleges and universities in the USA, how are you going to choose which ones to explore? Think about your secondary school experience and your community—do you want a university experience that is similar or are you looking for something new? Size, setting, and focus sum up the main differences among schools and this is a good place to begin your research.

SIZE: Small, medium, and large schools each have distinct characteristics with student populations ranging from a few hundred to tens of thousands. Small schools typically offer greater access to faculty, small class sizes and a strong sense of community. Large universities typically offer more majors, a wider variety of extracurricular activities and clubs, research opportunities and graduate programs. Large universities are typically comprised of many colleges, making it possible to feel a part of a smaller community.

SETTING: Urban, suburban, and rural schools each offer a different experience. An urban school presents the opportunity to immerse oneself in a city. In fact, at some urban schools, there is no real boundary between the campus and the surrounding community. If you're looking for easy access to the arts or professional sports, internship opportunities or an off-campus job, then an urban school may be for you. Rural schools are generally self-contained and usually have a greater sense of community. If you like activities such as hiking, a rural school may be the perfect place to earn your degree while taking advantage of the setting. Suburban or small town schools combine a little bit of both. They tend to be self-contained but offer easy access to the surrounding community. Setting and geographic location within the USA influence the cost of living. Consider extending your search to include schools throughout the country to compare costs.

FOCUS: Focus refers to whether a school is considered a liberal arts college or a research or profession-oriented university. A liberal arts college typically offers a broad general curriculum, while a research or pre-professional university encourages an emphasis on a particular area of study. Other differences include: the range of majors and research opportunities, the proportion of classes taught by professors, teaching assistants or graduate students, and graduate study opportunities. Focus is an important factor when considering what type of school you'd like to attend.

PUBLIC vs PRIVATE: The major difference between public and private schools is how they are funded. The cost of operating public universities is paid for by student tuition and by the government in the state in which they are located. The majority of the costs of running private colleges and universities are covered by student tuition and private donations. As a result, tuition is usually lower at public universities. Generally, public universities are large in size and in-state residents make up the majority of the student population.

There are so many resources available to help you explore your options.

GUIDEBOOKS AND ONLINE RESOURCES

➤ Start with college guidebooks; these offer facts about basic admission requirements, including academic average or GPA, SAT and ACT ranges, and course prerequisites. You'll also find information about tuition, graduation rates, student body, demographics and feedback from current students and alumni. Look up the profile of the incoming class to find the most up-to-date statistics.

➤ Read free online college resource guides that provide student-written reviews, tools to compare affordability, and rankings. While you read about rankings, keep in mind there is no "official" ranking system in the USA.

➤ Use online search sites to find schools that match your profile and interests.

➤ Follow college admissions related blogs which offer tips, reminders, resources, and admissions news.

➤ Look through school websites to learn more about a school's student body, required curriculum, course offerings, majors, admissions requirements, tuition and financial aid, housing, and extracurricular activities.

➤ Take virtual tours of campuses and browse through online photo galleries to get a sense of a school's physical setting.

➤ Search online for virtual college fairs and webinars offered by a number of government agencies and private organizations.

➤ Use social networking sites to connect with current students, faculty, and admission reps, as well as with other applicants.

COLLEGE FAIRS AND COLLEGE REP VISITS

College fairs bring together many colleges and universities in one place, offering you a very efficient way to gather information for your college search. These events are also a great way to meet American admissions reps. Attend these events to learn more about schools you're interested in, gain exposure to schools you may not be familiar with, connect with admissions reps and get answers to your questions. This is a great way to start your college search. With advanced planning, you can get the most out of college fairs.

> ➤ Start researching college fairs by looking online and check with your school counselor for a complete schedule of fairs in your area.

> ➤ Once you've identified fairs you'd like to attend, register online and in advance, if possible.

> ➤ Get ready to attend the fair by reviewing the list of participating schools and deciding which reps you'd like to meet and which events you'd like to attend. Prepare by thinking about what type of school may be the best for you: two-or four-year, size, setting, special programs and areas of study. Have a few talking points ready for when you meet with college reps at their booths.

> ➤ Plan your day. When you arrive, pick up a map and jot down the start times of special events. Begin with the schools at the top of your list, but keep an open mind as you walk through the aisles and stop in to look at a variety of schools and chat with their reps. Take brochures and course catalogs to review later when you have more time.

> ➤ Don't forget to ask for business cards after your conversations so you can follow up. Reach out if you have any additional questions.

Also, you may want to send a thank you note or email if you felt you had a meaningful conversation.

➢ Get organized. Sort through the brochures and business cards you collected and save the ones you're interested in. Go online, look further into the schools you liked and create a preliminary list of schools you're interested in.

College admissions representatives visit secondary schools throughout the world. At these visits, reps talk about what their school has to offer and provide details about their specific admissions requirements. Meeting your admissions rep in a small group setting presents a great opportunity for you to make a connection and establish a relationship with one of the individuals who may be reading your application. This is just one way to demonstrate your interest in a particular school. Demonstrated interest is a measure used by many colleges and universities to track a prospective student's interest in their school and the likelihood they would attend if admitted. Make every effort to attend visits by reps from schools you're genuinely interested in applying to, as demonstrated interest is often noted.

Prepare to meet with college reps at both fairs and at your school by having questions ready. Remember to ask only questions that cannot be answered on the school's website.

Questions you may want to ask a college rep:

- What is your school best known for?
- What are your strongest academic programs?
- What is the most popular major?
- How would you describe the personality of the student body?
- Where do most of the students come from?
- Do most students live on or off-campus?

- Is there an academic advisory system in place?

- Are academic tutors available?

- Are there internship opportunities available?

- Does the school help students with job placement after graduation?

ON-CAMPUS VISITS

Now, you'll hopefully have a better idea of what appeals to you. It's very possible that you have never been on a college campus in the USA. If your schedule and budget permit, plan a trip to get an up-close look at some of the schools you're considering. Given the travel distance to colleges and universities in the USA, campus visits may not be possible. So keep in mind, there are many other ways to learn more about the schools you're interested in, including virtual tours and conversations with your admissions rep.

It's ideal to visit when school is in session. Most colleges still offer tours during school vacation, but there may be fewer students to see and talk to. Your counselor can also help you make an initial list of schools to visit.

Keep in mind that you may be able to stay with a student on campus. If you don't know a student who can be your host, many schools will make arrangements for you. Contact the admissions office for details. Check the school website for travel resources, including information on local hotels, restaurants, attractions and transportation options.

Look through the admissions sections of school websites for info session and campus tour schedules, and don't miss the opportunity to get a full look at all each school has to offer. Check whether reservations are required and, if so, book online or by calling the admissions office. Once you arrive, don't forget to sign in. Some schools do take note of an applicant's interest in the school and your visit will speak to your desire to attend.

> **"I would also tell students how important it is to demonstrate interest in the college they are applying to, especially if that school is a top choice. We will document if a student has interacted with our staff directly through email conversations, phone conversations, campus tours, information sessions, and personal interviews with a staff member."**
>
> **—NICOLE KELMAN, Assistant Director of Admission, Muhlenberg College**

Info sessions give you the chance to learn about the school from Admissions staff who will make a formal presentation, followed by Q&A. Ask questions, but ask only those that are not addressed on the school's website.

Questions to ask at the admissions info session:

- What is the average class size?
- What mistakes do students make most often on their applications?
- What components must be in a student's file before you begin to read their application?
- Do you recommend sending supplemental material if a student has a special interest?
- What grabs your attention when you read an application?
- What percentage of classes are taught by full-time professors, adjunct (or part-time professors) or graduate student teaching assistants (TAs)?

- What type of financial assistance is available?

- What career service support is offered for summer and full-time opportunities?

- What jobs are available on campus for students who want to work part-time?

Campus tours are an essential part of a visit. Tours give you a look at what the facilities have to offer and a view into the school's personality. You'll see a school through a current student's eyes and have a chance to ask questions.

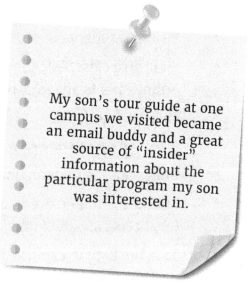

My son's tour guide at one campus we visited became an email buddy and a great source of "insider" information about the particular program my son was interested in.

Questions for your tour guide:

- Does the school provide housing for all four years? If yes, do most students stay on campus? If no, how hard is it to find off-campus housing?

- Are fraternities and sororities, commonly referred to as Greek life, an important component of the student body social life?

- What clubs and extracurriculars are offered?

- What's your favorite thing about the school? What, if anything, has disappointed you?

- How available are professors for extra help?

- Are tutors available?

- Is there a supportive advisory system? Are you assigned a freshman advisor?

- Do you feel safe on campus and in the surrounding area?

Explore the campus and spend time after the tour and info session engaging in campus life. Look around and take notice of what students are doing.

Things to do while you're on campus:

- Eat in the cafeteria.

- Visit the student center.

- Sit in on a class. Ask Admissions how to make arrangements ahead of time.

- Talk with students.

- Read the school newspaper.

- Check out the bulletin boards throughout campus.

- Attend an athletic event, a theatre production or a concert. Buy tickets ahead of time.

- Take the time to explore the surrounding neighborhood and town.

Reach out to any current students you know. They can answer the questions you don't want to pose on your tour and info session. Ask them to walk you through the parts of campus not covered on the tour, introduce you to their friends and maybe even show you their dorm or sorority or fraternity house.

Questions you can ask current students:

- Where do most students study?

- How much time do you spend on schoolwork each day?

- Do students stay on campus for the weekends?

- What do you do for fun?

- Do students feel pressured to join Greek life? What's the process like?

- What are the biggest campus traditions?

- Do students get involved in the surrounding community?

- What do you like best (and least) about the school?

- What is the security like on campus?

- How would you describe the students at the school?

Throughout the day, take notes and photos to help you remember details from your visit. Once you're back home, it'll be difficult to remember which school had the good food and where you noticed the students seemed the happiest. Use the worksheets provided in this chapter to record relevant information and help remind you of your reactions to the schools you investigate. 15 copies of each **School Search** worksheet are provided— use one for each school you research.

INTERVIEWS/MEETINGS

Interviews, whether on campus, at your school or via Skype, and meetings and calls with administrators, faculty, students and alumni are all part of the research and application process. These conversations offer a chance to learn more about a school, allow you to express your interest in attending and share something about yourself that's not revealed through your transcript, test scores, essays and activities. Contact each school to learn more about their interview policies and opportunities.

Prepare in advance so you'll feel more relaxed and in control. Consider doing the following:

> Get ready for your interview by reading through the school's website. The interview is your opportunity to show that you've done your homework. You'll also have the chance to ask questions

and learn more about the school. Think of questions in advance; a few possibilities are:

> Can you tell me about the _____ department? I'm thinking of that as my major.

> Will I be assigned an academic advisor?

> Are there any special programs that would suit my background and interests?

> How does course registration work? Is it difficult to get into classes?

> Are there any big plans or changes for the campus in the works?

➢ Be prepared to talk about yourself. Questions you may be asked include:

> Can you tell me something interesting about yourself?

> Why are you interested in attending?

> How do you plan to get involved in campus life?

> What accomplishment are you most proud of?

> What is your favorite book?

➢ An interview presents you with the chance to bring up anything in your record that you'd like to explain, such as a temporary drop in your grades. Prepare your answer and try it out on a family member.

➢ Remember to present your best self. Arrive a few minutes early, turn off your cell phone, shake hands, make eye contact and be confident.

Alumni interviews may be offered and/or required as well. Meetings with alumni are generally informal chats in a local coffee shop, public library or even in a classroom at your school. As with other interviews, this is a chance for you to have a conversation where you learn about the university from another perspective and where the university representative learns more about you. After you've applied, check the school's website to know whether an alum will contact you or whether you are responsible for scheduling an interview.

Meetings with faculty and athletic coaches are a chance to connect with a member of the school community who may be interested in your profile and who might provide you with additional information about programs that interest you. You may want to talk to a professor who teaches in the department you're considering, the coach of the team you'd like to join or a counselor in the career center. Schedule your meeting to coordinate with other events you'd like to attend on campus. If relevant, bring videos or samples of your work. Research their program ahead of time and prepare questions.

> **"Aim to maintain consistent communication with the colleges and universities of your choice. Build a relationship with the admissions officer that travels to your region. Set up interviews if possible. Speak with the representative at a fair or when they visit your high school; take their business card, and follow up. Visit, take a tour, and sit in on an information session. Attend Open Houses if they are available. If you cannot visit (i.e., distance) ask for an alumni interview."**
>
> **—ZEE SANTIAGO, Assistant Director of Admissions, Trinity College**

Ask each person you meet for their contact info and use an envelope to collect and save business cards. Remember to send thank you notes and to follow up if you've been asked to provide additional information. The people you meet during this investigative stage may be contacts you'll wish to reach out to later. In the early stages of the application process, your correspondence may be for fact-finding. However, as the process progresses, you may need to update your admissions file or contact a representative in support of your application. In addition, at a later date, take the opportunity to build a rapport with your admissions rep by reaching out with questions via email, Skype or FaceTime, or make a phone call using WhatsApp or Viber. Maintain a separate **Correspondence Journal** for each school you apply to. Enter the contact info for tour guides, admissions office representatives, professors and coaches. This log enables you to record the names and dates of your correspondence for easy and quick reference.

> "We welcome questions by either email or telephone, depending on what works best for you. Since high school students tend to be in school during regular business hours, many students find email to be a more practical way of reaching their counselors."
>
> —JIM ROGERS, Dean of Admission, Marymount Manhattan College

School Search

On-Campus Visit/Online Reasearch

TOUR GUIDE:

_____

Telephone: _____

Email: _____

INFORMATION SESSION LEADER:

_____

Telephone: _____

Email: _____

ADMISSIONS REGIONAL REPRESENTATIVE:

_____

Telephone: _____

Email: _____

Name of school:

Date of Campus Visit:

BASIC FACTS

Community (circle):   urban   suburban   rural

Surrounding neighborhood: _____

Accessibility (circle): car   train   plane

Transportation Costs: _____   Average total cost per year: _____

Your estimated cost to attend: _____

(use the **NET PRICE CALCULATOR** on the school's website)

FACILITIES

Housing options (singles, doubles, suites) (co-ed?) (guaranteed for 4 years?):

Dining halls:

Student center:

Athletic facilities/fitness center:

Cultural event space (theatres, galleries...):

Student health services:

Buildings and grounds:

Look around! If time allows, have lunch at a dining hall. Are students socializing, are they engaged in conversations, or are they studying?

STUDENT BODY

Size: _____

Male/female ratio: _____

Diversity: _____

Academic atmosphere: _____

School spirit: _____

Personality (friendly, helpful...): _____

Undergraduate versus graduate population: _____

Average SAT score:_____

Average ACT score:_____

Average GPA:_____

Try to strike up a conversation with a current student.

ACADEMICS

Student-faculty ratio:

_____

Classes taught by professors vs teaching assistants:

_____

Average class size:

_____

Classrooms/labs/support facilities:

_____

Popular majors/programs:

_____

Library(ies):

_____

Availability of tutoring:

_____

Advisory support:

_____

Career counseling/placement:

_____

If you attend a class, try to chat with the professor before or after.

EXTRACURRICULAR ACTIVITIES

Greek life:

_____

_____

Clubs:

_____

_____

Athletics (club, intramural):

_____

_____

Availability of religous services:

_____

_____

Community service opportunities:

_____

_____

Cultural events:

_____

_____

Other activities that interest you:

_____

_____

_____

_____

Notable points made by
admissions representatives:

_____
_____
_____
_____
_____
_____
_____
_____

What did you learn from your tour guide?

Outstanding memories:

Reasons you're interested in this school:

_____
_____
_____
_____
_____
_____
_____
_____

School Search

On-Campus Visit/Online Reasearch

TOUR GUIDE:

_____

Telephone: _____

Email: _____

INFORMATION SESSION LEADER:

_____

Telephone: _____

Email: _____

ADMISSIONS REGIONAL REPRESENTATIVE:

_____

Telephone: _____

Email: _____

Name of school:

Date of Campus Visit:

BASIC FACTS

Community (circle):   urban   suburban   rural

Surrounding neighborhood: _____

Accessibility (circle):   car   train   plane

Transportation Costs: _____   Average total cost per year: _____

Your estimated cost to attend: _____

(use the **NET PRICE CALCULATOR** on the school's website)

FACILITIES

Housing options (singles, doubles, suites) (co-ed?) (guaranteed for 4 years?):

Dining halls:

Student center:

Athletic facilities/fitness center:

Cultural event space (theatres, galleries...):

Student health services:

Buildings and grounds:

Look around! If time allows, have lunch at a dining hall. Are students socializing, are they engaged in conversations, or are they studying?

STUDENT BODY

Size: _____

Male/female ratio: _____

Diversity: _____

Academic atmosphere: _____

School spirit: _____

Personality (friendly, helpful...): _____

Undergraduate versus graduate population: _____

Try to strike up a conversation with a current student.

Average SAT score:_____

Average ACT score:_____

Average GPA:_____

ACADEMICS

Student-faculty ratio:

_____

Classes taught by professors vs teaching assistants:

_____

Average class size:

_____

Classrooms/labs/support facilities:

_____

Popular majors/programs:

_____

Library(ies):

_____

Availability of tutoring:

_____

Advisory support:

_____

Career counseling/placement:

_____

If you attend a class, try to chat with the professor before or after.

EXTRACURRICULAR ACTIVITIES

Greek life:

_____

_____

Clubs:

_____

_____

Athletics (club, intramural):

_____

_____

Availability of religous services:

_____

_____

Community service opportunities:

_____

_____

Cultural events:

_____

_____

Other activities that interest you:

_____

_____

_____

_____

Notable points made by
admissions representatives:

_____

_____

_____

_____

_____

_____

_____

_____

What did you learn from your tour guide?

Outstanding memories:

Reasons you're interested in this school:

_____

_____

_____

_____

_____

_____

_____

School Search

On-Campus Visit/Online Reasearch

TOUR GUIDE:

_____

Telephone: _____

Email: _____

INFORMATION SESSION LEADER:

_____

Telephone: _____

Email: _____

ADMISSIONS REGIONAL REPRESENTATIVE:

_____

Telephone: _____

Email: _____

Name of school:

Date of Campus Visit:

BASIC FACTS

Community (circle):   urban   suburban   rural

Surrounding neighborhood: _____

Accessibility (circle): car   train   plane

Transportation Costs: _____   Average total cost per year: _____

Your estimated cost to attend: _____

(use the **NET PRICE CALCULATOR** on the school's website)

FACILITIES

Housing options (singles, doubles, suites) (co-ed?) (guaranteed for 4 years?):

Dining halls:

Student center:

Athletic facilities/fitness center:

Cultural event space (theatres, galleries...):

Student health services:

Buildings and grounds:

> Look around! If time allows, have lunch at a dining hall. Are students socializing, are they engaged in conversations, or are they studying?

STUDENT BODY

Size: _____

Male/female ratio: _____

Diversity: _____

Academic atmosphere: _____

School spirit: _____

Personality (friendly, helpful...): _____

Undergraduate versus graduate population: _____

> Try to strike up a conversation with a current student.

Average SAT score:_____

Average ACT score:_____

Average GPA:_____

ACADEMICS

Student-faculty ratio:

_____

Classes taught by professors vs teaching assistants:

_____

Average class size:

_____

Classrooms/labs/support facilities:

_____

Popular majors/programs:

_____

Library(ies):

_____

Availability of tutoring:

_____

Advisory support:

_____

Career counseling/placement:

_____

If you attend a class, try to chat with the professor before or after.

EXTRACURRICULAR ACTIVITIES

Greek life:

_____

_____

Clubs:

_____

_____

Athletics (club, intramural):

_____

_____

Availability of religous services:

_____

_____

Community service opportunities:

_____

_____

Cultural events:

_____

_____

Other activities that interest you:

_____

_____

_____

_____

Notable points made by
admissions representatives:

_____

_____

_____

_____

_____

_____

_____

What did you learn from your tour guide?

Outstanding memories:

Reasons you're interested in this school:

_____

_____

_____

_____

_____

_____

_____

_____

School Search

On-Campus Visit/Online Reasearch

TOUR GUIDE:

_____

Telephone: _____

Email: _____

INFORMATION SESSION LEADER:

_____

Telephone: _____

Email: _____

ADMISSIONS REGIONAL REPRESENTATIVE:

_____

Telephone: _____

Email: _____

Name of school:

Date of Campus Visit:

BASIC FACTS

Community (circle):   urban   suburban   rural

Surrounding neighborhood: _____

Accessibility (circle):   car   train   plane

Transportation Costs: _____   Average total cost per year: _____

Your estimated cost to attend: _____

(use the **NET PRICE CALCULATOR** on the school's website)

FACILITIES

Housing options (singles, doubles, suites) (co-ed?) (guaranteed for 4 years?):

Dining halls:

Student center:

Athletic facilities/fitness center:

Cultural event space (theatres, galleries...):

Student health services:

Buildings and grounds:

Look around! If time allows, have lunch at a dining hall. Are students socializing, are they engaged in conversations, or are they studying?

STUDENT BODY

Size: _____

Male/female ratio: _____

Diversity: _____

Academic atmosphere: _____

School spirit: _____

Personality (friendly, helpful...): _____

Undergraduate versus graduate population: _____

Try to strike up a conversation with a current student.

Average SAT score:_____

Average ACT score:_____

Average GPA:_____

ACADEMICS

Student-faculty ratio:

_____

Classes taught by professors vs teaching assistants:

_____

Average class size:

_____

Classrooms/labs/support facilities:

_____

Popular majors/programs:

_____

Library(ies):

_____

Availability of tutoring:

_____

Advisory support:

_____

Career counseling/placement:

_____

If you attend a class, try to chat with the professor before or after.

EXTRACURRICULAR ACTIVITIES

Greek life:

_____

_____

Clubs:

_____

_____

Athletics (club, intramural):

_____

_____

Availability of religous services:

_____

_____

Community service opportunities:

_____

_____

Cultural events:

_____

_____

Other activities that interest you:

_____

_____

_____

_____

Notable points made by
admissions representatives:

_____

_____

_____

_____

_____

_____

_____

_____

What did you learn from your tour guide?

Outstanding memories:

Reasons you're interested in this school:

_____

_____

_____

_____

_____

_____

_____

_____

_____

School Search

On-Campus Visit/Online Reasearch

TOUR GUIDE:

_____

Telephone: _____

Email: _____

INFORMATION SESSION LEADER:

_____

Telephone: _____

Email: _____

ADMISSIONS REGIONAL REPRESENTATIVE:

_____

Telephone: _____

Email: _____

Name of school:

Date of Campus Visit:

BASIC FACTS

Community (circle):   urban   suburban   rural

Surrounding neighborhood: _____

Accessibility (circle): car   train   plane

Transportation Costs: _____   Average total cost per year: _____

Your estimated cost to attend: _____

(use the **NET PRICE CALCULATOR** on the school's website)

FACILITIES

Housing options (singles, doubles, suites) (co-ed?) (guaranteed for 4 years?):

Dining halls:

Student center:

Athletic facilities/fitness center:

Cultural event space (theatres, galleries...):

Student health services:

Buildings and grounds:

Look around! If time allows, have lunch at a dining hall. Are students socializing, are they engaged in conversations, or are they studying?

STUDENT BODY

Size: _____

Male/female ratio: _____

Diversity: _____

Academic atmosphere: _____

School spirit: _____

Personality (friendly, helpful...): _____

Undergraduate versus graduate population: _____

Try to strike up a conversation with a current student.

Average SAT score:_____

Average ACT score:_____

Average GPA:_____

ACADEMICS

Student-faculty ratio:

_____

Classes taught by professors vs teaching assistants:

_____

Average class size:

_____

Classrooms/labs/support facilities:

_____

Popular majors/programs:

_____

Library(ies):

_____

Availability of tutoring:

_____

Advisory support:

_____

Career counseling/placement:

_____

If you attend a class, try to chat with the professor before or after.

EXTRACURRICULAR ACTIVITIES

Greek life:

_____

_____

Clubs:

_____

_____

Athletics (club, intramural):

_____

_____

Availability of religous services:

_____

_____

Community service opportunities:

_____

_____

Cultural events:

_____

_____

Other activities that interest you:

_____

_____

_____

_____

Notable points made by
admissions representatives:

_____

_____

_____

_____

_____

_____

_____

_____

What did you learn from your tour guide?

Outstanding memories:

Reasons you're interested in this school:

_____

_____

_____

_____

_____

_____

_____

_____

ON-CAMPUS MEETINGS

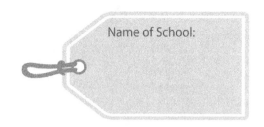

Name of School:

Name: Position:

Telephone number: Date/Time:

Email:

Locations:

Notable information/ impressions:

Remember: Send a thank you note to each person you meet.

Enter all correspondence in your journal!

Name: Position:

Telephone number: Date/Time:

Email:

Locations:

Notable information/ impressions:

Name: Position:

Telephone number: Date/Time:

Email:

Locations:

Notable information/ impressions:

ON-CAMPUS MEETINGS

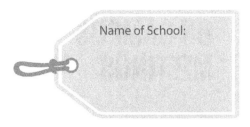

Name of School:

Name: Position:

Telephone number: Date/Time:

Email:

Locations:

Notable information/ impressions:

Remember: Send a thank you note to each person you meet.

Enter all correspondence in your journal!

Name: Position:

Telephone number: Date/Time:

Email:

Locations:

Notable information/ impressions:

Name: Position:

Telephone number: Date/Time:

Email:

Locations:

Notable information/ impressions:

ON-CAMPUS MEETINGS

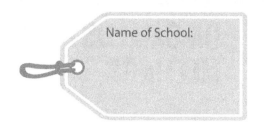

Name of School:

Name: Position:

Telephone number: Date/Time:

Email:

Locations:

Notable information/ impressions:

Remember: Send a thank you note to each person you meet.

Enter all correspondence in your journal!

Name: Position:

Telephone number: Date/Time:

Email:

Locations:

Notable information/ impressions:

Name: Position:

Telephone number: Date/Time:

Email:

Locations:

Notable information/ impressions:

ON-CAMPUS MEETINGS

Name of School:

Name: Position:

Telephone number: Date/Time:

Email:

Locations:

Notable information/ impressions:

Remember: Send a thank you note to each person you meet.

Enter all correspondence in your journal!

Name: Position:

Telephone number: Date/Time:

Email:

Locations:

Notable information/ impressions:

Name: Position:

Telephone number: Date/Time:

Email:

Locations:

Notable information/ impressions:

ON-CAMPUS MEETINGS

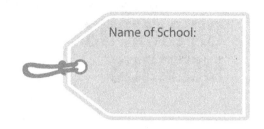

Name of School:

Name: Position:

Telephone number: Date/Time:

Email:

Locations:

Notable information/ impressions:

Remember: Send a thank you note to each person you meet.

Enter all correspondence in your journal!

Name: Position:

Telephone number: Date/Time:

Email:

Locations:

Notable information/ impressions:

Name: Position:

Telephone number: Date/Time:

Email:

Locations:

Notable information/ impressions:

ON-CAMPUS MEETINGS

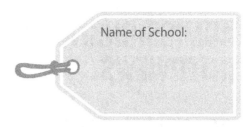

Name of School:

Name: Position:

Telephone number: Date/Time:

Email:

Locations:

Notable information/ impressions:

Remember: Send a thank you note to each person you meet.

Enter all correspondence in your journal!

Name: Position:

Telephone number: Date/Time:

Email:

Locations:

Notable information/ impressions:

Name: Position:

Telephone number: Date/Time:

Email:

Locations:

Notable information/ impressions:

ADMISSIONS/ALUMNI INTERVIEWS

Name of School:

ADMISSIONS INTERVIEW

Name: Date/Time:

Email: Telephone number:

Notable information:

ALUMNI INTERVIEW

Name: Date/Time:

Email: Telephone number:

Notable information:

Did you send a thank you note? Remember to enter the note in your **Correspondence Journal**

ADMISSIONS/ALUMNI INTERVIEWS

Name of School:

ADMISSIONS INTERVIEW

Name: Date/Time:

Email: Telephone number:

Notable information:

ALUMNI INTERVIEW

Name: Date/Time:

Email: Telephone number:

Notable information:

Did you send a thank you note? Remember to enter the note in your **Correspondence Journal**

ADMISSIONS/ALUMNI INTERVIEWS

Name of School:

ADMISSIONS INTERVIEW

Name: Date/Time:

Email: Telephone number:

Notable information:

ALUMNI INTERVIEW

Name: Date/Time:

Email: Telephone number:

Notable information:

Did you send a thank you note? Remember to enter the note in your **Correspondence Journal**

ADMISSIONS/ALUMNI INTERVIEWS

Name of School:

ADMISSIONS INTERVIEW

Name: Date/Time:

Email: Telephone number:

Notable information:

ALUMNI INTERVIEW

Name: Date/Time:

Email: Telephone number:

Notable information:

Did you send a thank you note? Remember to enter the note in your **Correspondence Journal**

ADMISSIONS/ALUMNI INTERVIEWS

Name of School:

ADMISSIONS INTERVIEW

Name: Date/Time:

Email: Telephone number:

Notable information:

ALUMNI INTERVIEW

Name: Date/Time:

Email: Telephone number:

Notable information:

Did you send a thank you note? Remember to enter the note in your **Correspondence Journal**

ADMISSIONS/ALUMNI INTERVIEWS

Name of School:

ADMISSIONS INTERVIEW

Name: Date/Time:

Email: Telephone number:

Notable information:

ALUMNI INTERVIEW

Name: Date/Time:

Email: Telephone number:

Notable information:

Did you send a thank you note? Remember to enter the note in your **Correspondence Journal**

CORRESPONDENCE JOURNAL

Name of School:

DATE	TYPE*	CONTACT NAME	REGARDING

*Type of correspondence: email, letter, telephone call

CORRESPONDENCE JOURNAL

Name of School:

DATE	TYPE*	CONTACT NAME	REGARDING

*Type of correspondence: email, letter, telephone call

CORRESPONDENCE JOURNAL

Name of School:

DATE	TYPE*	CONTACT NAME	REGARDING

*Type of correspondence: email, letter, telephone call

CORRESPONDENCE JOURNAL

Name of School:

DATE	TYPE*	CONTACT NAME	REGARDING

*Type of correspondence: email, letter, telephone call

CORRESPONDENCE JOURNAL

Name of School:

DATE	TYPE*	CONTACT NAME	REGARDING

*Type of correspondence: email, letter, telephone call

CORRESPONDENCE JOURNAL

Name of School:

DATE	TYPE*	CONTACT NAME	REGARDING

*Type of correspondence: email, letter, telephone call

CORRESPONDENCE JOURNAL

Name of School:

DATE	TYPE*	CONTACT NAME	REGARDING

*Type of correspondence: email, letter, telephone call

CORRESPONDENCE JOURNAL

Name of School:

DATE	TYPE*	CONTACT NAME	REGARDING

*Type of correspondence: email, letter, telephone call

CORRESPONDENCE JOURNAL

Name of School:

DATE	TYPE*	CONTACT NAME	REGARDING

*Type of correspondence: email, letter, telephone call

CORRESPONDENCE JOURNAL

Name of School:

DATE	TYPE*	CONTACT NAME	REGARDING

*Type of correspondence: email, letter, telephone call

CHAPTER 5

DEFINE YOUR CHOICES: YOU'RE READY TO APPLY!

YOUR FINAL LIST

Consolidating your preliminary list may seem like an impossible task because no one school seems to meet all of your criteria. Use the information you've gathered from campus visits, info sessions, interviews, meetings, individual college websites, virtual tours, online resources, and your school's academic counseling department to identify the schools that are truly the best fit for you. Think back to how you felt on campus and during virtual tours. What was your reaction? Try to recall what you observed. Can you see yourself there for the next four years?

Seek advice from people who understand the college process and who also understand who you are and what you're capable of. Review your choices with your parents and counselor to get their input so they can help you compile a final list of about ten schools that meet both your academic and personal requirements. Develop a balanced list, including a mix of safety, reach, and target schools, both academically and financially. The current cost to attend can be obtained on school websites. The cost to attend includes tuition and fees, room and board, personal expenses, books and supplies, and travel. In the end, successful admissions are the result of both a good list and well-executed applications. In this chapter, you'll learn more about how to create a balanced final list, how to submit your applications, and how to manage multiple deadlines.

Using up-to-date admissions statistics for the most recently admitted students, provided on school websites, will help you refine your list. Academic safety schools include those schools where your grades and standardized test scores are in the upper end of the ranges of students applying and where you are likely to be admitted. Target schools are those schools where your grades and scores are in the mid-range of accepted students. Reach schools are typically schools that accept students whose academic credentials are generally higher than yours. Be sure that all the schools on your list are "good fit" schools, schools where you see yourself being happy and comfortable attending.

There are many variables affecting admissions decisions. Your best possible outcomes will result from identifying schools that are looking for students with your profile. The most objective of the admissions criteria are grades and test scores; however, the subjective factors of your college application are what set you apart from your peers and can tip a decision in your favor. Your special interests, talents and achievements make you a unique individual. Your recommendations offer a glimpse of the impression you've made on others. Additionally, your essays add your own voice to your application. Your demographics, including where you come from and the makeup of your secondary school class, provide the context in which admissions reps read your application. The interest you've demonstrated speaks to your desire to attend their school. It's also helpful to know how previous applicants from your school have fared in the admissions process at each school on your list.

As you can see, admissions decisions are based on many criteria which change from year to year. There is no way to predict future admissions decisions and there are no guarantees in college admissions. This is why it is essential for you to apply to a range of schools appropriate for your profile.

APPLYING

Once you have a final list of schools, you're ready to apply. A college application is comprised of many components and the accurate execution of each step is required to produce the best application possible. In the end, your application should reflect your best efforts.

> **"Students and families need to read the fine print, not assume anything! Even among similar institutions there will be different deadlines, requirements, etc."**
>
> **—NANCY HARGRAVE MEISLAHN, Dean of Admission and Financial Aid, Wesleyan University**

There is more than one way to apply to college. The Common Application is the most widely used application available online and in print.

In addition, there are a number of other applications accepted including individual college applications, the Universal College Application and the QuestBridge Application. Refer to college websites to confirm how to apply.

The Common App is an undergraduate application accepted by a vast number of American colleges and universities. You may open your Common App account at any time, work on your application and save it until it's ready for submission it to any participating school. You can also create multiple versions of the Common App. For example, you may want to tailor your essay to reference a

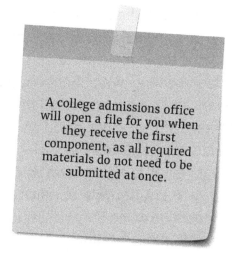

A college admissions office will open a file for you when they receive the first component, as all required materials do not need to be submitted at once.

specific program, professor or course. Many schools allow you to choose either the Common App or their own application; some require one or the other. Also, some schools require a supplement in addition to the Common App or individual school application. The supplement is typically an additional essay(s) and/or short answers. These requirements may be found on the Common App and individual school websites.

When creating your online accounts for the Common App and any of the other applications noted on page 129, don't forget to jot down your usernames and passwords on your **Student's Personal Information** worksheet on page 14. Once you open an account, read through the application to get an idea of all the information that will be required. You'll begin by providing basic facts about yourself and your family. The completed worksheets from Chapter 1 will help you to easily and accurately fill in this section.

While you're signed in to your Common App account, read the essay prompts and start thinking about how you will want to respond. Identify any additional essays you may be required to write. Supplemental essays for Common App schools can be found on the Common App or in individual school websites. Schools that have their own applications will have their essay topics posted on their website. Reduce your workload by looking at all the essay topics in advance. The objective of your essay should be to reveal something that isn't in your transcript or test scores. It's not the topic you choose, but how you relate it to your life experiences. You don't need to write about anything exotic or abstract. A topic that's ordinary and everyday can still help tell your own unique story, if you do it in a thoughtful way. While you want your essay to be well written, it needs to be authentic. It's okay to seek out help from a proofreader, but make sure your essay is in your own voice. Admissions officers want to hear what you have to say, not your parent, teacher or mentor. Give them a reason to remember you when they're sitting around the conference table deciding which candidates to admit.

"Check your spelling!!!"

—PAUL W. HORGAN, Director of College Counseling, Cape Henry
   Collegiate School, Virginia Beach, Virginia

**"The reality is that we do expect students to follow our application
instructions with great detail."**

—SHAWN ABBOTT, Assistant Vice President for Admissions,
   New York University

The colleges and universities you apply to want to get to know more about who you are and what you've accomplished. The Common App and individual school applications will ask you to list all the activities you've participated in during your secondary school years in order of importance to you. Now is the time to refer to the worksheets you completed in Chapter 2.

Supplementary materials, including art portfolios, music samples, videos and science research abstracts, to name a few, can enhance a strong application and may help tip the admissions decision in your favor. However, use discretion when deciding whether to send additional information in support of your application. Think about how many applications, including essays, test scores, activities lists and recommendations admissions

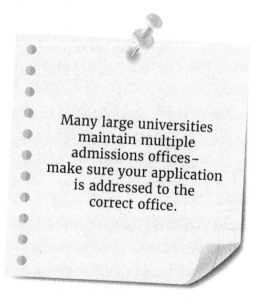

Many large universities maintain multiple admissions offices— make sure your application is addressed to the correct office.

officers are sorting through. Be sure what you submit is of the highest caliber and will enhance your profile. If you're not confident about what to do, it may be helpful to ask your academic counselor for input. In addition, confirm each individual school's policy regarding the submission of supplementary materials and follow the required format for submission by checking on the school's website and confirming the correct address.

> **"CVs and resumes are great if more explanation for the activities is needed. If the resume is just a listing of activities and no explanation, then it is just another piece of paper to look at."**
>
> **—Andrea Buchanan, Senior Assistant Director of Admissions, Coordinator for International Student Admissions, Gettysburg College**

Throughout your college application process you'll create many documents. You may need to write one or two essays for the Common App and possibly several more to meet individual school requirements. Consideration for special programs and scholarships calls for even more essays. To that, add the supporting documents demonstrating your involvement in specific academic and/or extracurricular activities. Think about the countless hours dedicated to composing this material. You'll write and rewrite, edit and then edit some more, and then proofread until, finally, your work is ready to be submitted.

Imagine if your work was inadvertently lost. Things can go wrong with your computer…viruses, failed hard drives and even floods can result in a loss of data. Always backup your work. It's simple to do and there are multiple methods to choose from, including external hard drives, online storage solutions and USB flash drives, to

Always save your work on your data storage device!

name a few. Find the system that works for you, and get into the habit of backing up your documents each and every time you work on your applications.

DEADLINES

Colleges and universities offer a variety of admissions options, each with a different deadline. Be sure you understand all the different application choices and are aware of all the relevant deadlines for each school on your list. Deadlines vary not only from school to school, but also within a school. Please be aware of different due dates for special programs and scholarships.

EARLY DECISION (ED) deadlines tend to be early to mid-November, with decisions being released in mid-December. If accepted, early decision admission is binding, so make sure you're ready to commit. If you require financial aid to attend and would like the opportunity to compare aid packages from all the schools that admit you, then early decision may not be right for you. Admission rates for early decision candidates are generally higher than for students who apply regular decision, since an early decision application conveys eagerness to attend. While this willingness to commit may improve your odds, you need to be confident this is the right school for you. You can only choose one school to apply ED.

EARLY DECISION II (ED II) deadlines are around January 1st with notifications in mid-February. This option is offered by some schools and acceptance is binding. You can only choose one school to apply to as an ED II applicant.

EARLY ACTION (EA) requires you to typically submit your application by early to mid-November, with results being released by mid-December. EA allows you to demonstrate your interest in being admitted to a school without having to make the binding commitment that ED imposes.

EA policies vary from school to school. Restrictive EA schools do not allow applicants to apply EA or ED elsewhere, while non-restrictive EA schools do allow students to submit EA or ED applications to other schools.

ROLLING DECISION schools review applications on an ongoing basis, where the application process typically opens in early fall and may continue as late as summer or as long as spaces are available. Applicants are notified of their outcome as applications are processed, so applying as early as possible may improve your chances of acceptance. While there may be no application deadline, there typically are due dates for scholarships, financial aid and housing.

REGULAR DECISION deadlines vary from school to school, but are usually between January 1 and mid-February. Decisions are typically released mid-March through early April.

OPEN DECISION is an option offered by community colleges and many online school programs to most secondary school graduates and equivalency certificate holders. Open decision schools accept students until all spaces in the incoming class are full.

SUBMITTING APPLICATIONS

You have your final list, you've determined what type of application to submit to each school and have reviewed your deadline options. Completing and submitting university applications is a huge undertaking with so many moving parts. You absolutely need to stay organized in order to accurately meet deadlines, avoid mistakes, monitor your applications and respond to further requests for information.

Please read and reread your Common App and essays; then ask a parent, teacher or friend to read through them as well. Use the "Print Preview" feature of the Common App to proofread your entire application before pressing the "Submit" button.

> "This is your process–take ownership and follow up with your colleges. Pay attention to deadlines."
>
> —**MARIA LAPINS, Senior Assistant Director of Admission, University of Richmond**

You will be responsible for creating, submitting and keeping track of every component of each application. Add to that, all the documents being sent by your recommenders, the testing services and your school's counseling office, to name a few. The **APPLICATION CHECKLIST** worksheet in the back of this chapter will be your go-to spreadsheet from the day you decide on your final list until the day you confirm that each school has received all your application components.

The **APPLICATION CHECKLIST** includes:

- ✓ SCHOOL: Fill in the name of each school.

- ✓ DUE DATE: Indicate whether you've chosen to apply for ED, EA, regular or rolling admission, along with the deadline.

- ✓ APPLICATION TYPE: Choose either the Common App, the Universal College Application, the QuestBridge Application or the school's own application and mark the box if a supplement is required.

- ✓ ADDITIONAL MATERIALS: Check "D" (for done), if and when you submit any supplementary materials in support of your applications.

- ✓ TEST SCORES: Check "D" when you request your scores be submitted for standardised tests.

- ✓ SCHOOL COUNSELOR: Your school counseling department will be submitting your transcript, a letter of recommendation and your mid-year grades.

✓ RECOMMENDATIONS: Provide your recommenders with your list of schools and then check "D" when done.

✓ FINANCIAL AID: For each school, check "D" when you're done submitting your CSS/Financial Aid PROFILE.

✓ FEE: Check this box when the application fee has been paid.

✓ DONE: Check this box after you've confirmed all components have been received, as you will be instructed in Chapter 7.

"Keeping tabs on letters and emails, tracking deadlines, and scheduling tasks is essential for success."

—LAURA A. BRUNO, Associate Director of Admissions, York College, The City University of New York

"Just keep in mind that, just as you have the option of contacting us via phone or email, our counselors will be trying to reach you through both media as well. Be sure to check your email and voicemail regularly for important messages throughout the application process."

—JIM ROGERS, Dean of Admission, Marymount Manhattan College

FOLDER SETUP

As you now see, there is a tremendous amount of information to manage as you apply to university. Although much of your work is done online, print hard copies of your documents for future reference, proof of submission or follow-up. Label three folders as follows:

Application folder—Include in this folder:

- ✓ a copy of your completed Common App, with essays , or any other completed application
- ✓ copies of individual school applications, including essays
- ✓ copies of any submission confirmations, if applicable

General folder—Fill this folder with:

- ✓ testing admission tickets
- ✓ score reports
- ✓ transcripts
- ✓ writing samples

Financial Aid / Scholarship folder (optional)—Include in this folder:

- ✓ a copy of your CSS/Financial Aid PROFILE
- ✓ a copy of any other submitted forms, corresponding essays and confirmations

APPLICATION CHECKLIST

SCHOOL NAME	DUE DATE	APPLICATIONS								SCORES												
		COMMON APP		SCHOOL		SUPPLEMENT		ADDITIONAL MATERIALS		ACT		SAT		SAT II		SAT II		SAT II		TOEFL/ IELTS	
		D	R	D	R	D	R	D	R	D	R	D	R	D	R	D	R	D	R	D	R

APPLICATION CHECKLIST

SCHOOL NAME	SCHOOL COUNSELOR						RECOMMENDATIONS						FINANCIAL AID						FEE	DONE
	TRANSCRIPT		LETTER		MID YEAR GRADES		1		2		3		COF		CSS/PROFILE					
	D	R	D	R	D	R	D	R	D	R	D	R	D	R	D	R				

CHAPTER 6

PAYING THE BILLS: FINDING THE FUNDS

Tuition and fees differ from school to school. Factors impacting your cost to attend include the location of a school and whether it is public or private. Check school websites for details on the cost to attend.

You and your family may have already discussed how you will pay for university. Remember that the total cost to attend includes tuition and fees, room and board, personal expenses, books and supplies, and travel. Keep in mind that the cost to attend generally increases annually.

International applicants must verify their ability to pay in order to attend university in the USA. College Board's International Student Certification of Finances (COF) is the form most commonly used by colleges and universities. This form is also used by schools to issue a Certificate of Eligibility (Form I-20 or DS-2019) to accepted students which is necessary when applying for a student visa. College Board's International Student Financial Aid Application form may also be required. It is essential to check with each school, either on their website or by contacting your admissions rep directly, to verify requirements.

Financial aid money is available from a number of sources, including the college or university you attend and both nonprofit and private organizations. The availability of financial aid is school specific and so it is a good idea to reach out to the financial aid office at each school you're considering to discuss funding available to international students. You won't know how much aid you will be offered until after you apply, so apply to both financial target and reach schools to keep your options open until you have all your admissions decisions and aid packages in hand. Use the Net Price Calculator by going on individual school websites or visit the United States Department of Education's online Net Price Calculator Center.

> **"If you want to go to college this fall, you absolutely can afford to go to college! The key is for students to stay open-minded about the thousands of colleges and universities that exist in the United States today; ranging from elite, high-priced private institutions to larger, public, low-priced community colleges. There isn't just one college out there for each student. There are hundreds. So every student can get admitted to college and every student can afford to go to college."**
>
> **—JACQUELYN NEALON, ED.D., Vice President, Enrollment, Communications and Marketing, New York Institute of Technology**

At first, the financial aid process may seem overwhelming, but the more you understand about the system, the more successful you will be in gaining aid.

TYPES OF FINANCIAL AID

LOANS are money you borrow for college that you must repay, with interest, each with its own repayment schedule.

- College and university sponsored loans may be a source of financial aid. Check with financial aid offices to determine availability.

- Private loans are available from a variety of lenders and other financial institutions, as well as private organizations and nonprofits. Borrowing terms vary and it's best to check with the lender for details.

GRANTS AND SCHOLARSHIPS are often called gift aid because they never have to be repaid. Included in this list are:

- Scholarships, which may be need or merit-based and are awarded through state, school and private groups and institutions.

- Grants, which also may be need or merit-based. Check with each school for details regarding college and university funded grants.

- Tuition waivers, which offer a type of financial aid in which the college or university waives all or part of tuition charges. Eligibility for tuition waivers may be linked to employment and are available to employees and their qualified dependents at schools offering such programs. Waivers may also be available to teaching assistants and resident advisors, to name a few.

WORK-STUDY programs offer students part-time jobs, usually on campus, to help meet financial need. Opportunities vary from school to school and hours are dictated by the conditions of your visa.

> **"Do not throw a school off your list just because the price may seem out of your range. You do not know what their scholarship structure is."**
>
> **—SUNIL SAMUEL, Director of Admission, Hofstra University**

APPLYING FOR FINANCIAL AID

The **Financial Aid Worksheet** provided in this chapter will help you with the challenging task of managing deadlines. In the financial aid world, applications have different deadlines and deadlines are absolute. There are no second chances. The key is to apply as early as possible, stay ahead of deadlines and respond quickly to requests for additional information.

> **"Families are often very focused on the application process and can forget about deadlines for the financial aid process. Late applications for financial aid are a huge mistake and cost families money in lost scholarships."**
>
> **—AMY BAUMGARTEL SINGER, Director of College Counseling, The Wheeler School, Providence, Rhode Island**

Colleges and universities require any number of forms in order to apply for aid. Check each individual school's website to determine which forms are required and note their respective deadlines on the **Financial Aid Worksheet**.

The most commonly required forms are CSS/Financial Aid PROFILE and individual school forms. CSS/PROFILE submits your aid applications directly to the schools you specify. Schools are identified by four-digit codes on the CSS/PROFILE. These codes are available on school websites, as well as on the CSS/PROFILE online sites. Get a head start on your aid applications and use the space provided in the worksheet to note the codes relevant to your applications.

CSS/FINANCIAL AID PROFILE

The CSS/PROFILE provides the information colleges and universities need to distribute need-based grants and scholarships. If you want to be considered, the CSS/PROFILE must be completed on College Board's website. You may not be sure you'll qualify for aid, and honestly, you won't know unless you apply. Each college and university has their own requirements for financial aid, scholarships and grant money. Check the financial aid section of each school's website or call the financial aid office directly to confirm their requirements.

You must register with College Board in order to complete the CSS/ PROFILE. If you already have a College Board account, use your username and password for the CSS/PROFILE as well. If not, record your new username and password on the **Student's Personal Information** worksheet provided in Chapter 1. After you've registered with College Board, look through the list of participating colleges and universities to determine if any of the schools on your list use the PROFILE as part of their financial aid process. Keep a list of each school's code and jot down the priority and closing filing dates on the **Financial Aid Worksheet**. Some aid is granted on a first-come, first-served basis; apply as early as allowed. Once you've registered, go to College Board's website to print and complete the pre-application worksheet and application instructions prior to working on your online CSS/PROFILE. You can finish the PROFILE in one sitting or save your work and return to it at a later time.

Once you submit a CSS/PROFILE, you will receive an Acknowledgment / Data Confirmation Report from College Board. The acknowledgment includes the data you entered on your application and the list of colleges to which you've chosen to send your financial aid information. Print and then file this acknowledgment in your **Financial Aid / Scholarship** folder. You may be asked to provide this to the school you choose to attend.

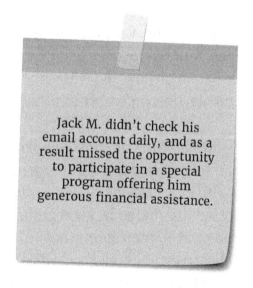

Jack M. didn't check his email account daily, and as a result missed the opportunity to participate in a special program offering him generous financial assistance.

It is not uncommon for individual schools to request additional information in support of your financial aid application. Some colleges or scholarship programs may request you provide additional documents through College Board's Institutional Documentation Service (IDOC). You will be sent notification from College Board if such information is needed. Check your email daily for important correspondence and be sure to reply immediately.

International Student Financial Aid Application (ISFAA)

The International Student Financial Aid Application (ISFAA) is available on College Board's website and is required by some colleges and universities from international students applying for aid.

SCHOLARSHIPS

Scholarships are available from individual colleges and universities as well as from private and public sources. Start searching for scholarships as early as possible in your application process. It may take time to complete applications since they often require essays and recommendations. There are many helpful websites and resources to help you find scholarship money. Your school counseling office should be your first stop for information on how and where to search for scholarships. Ask for a list of legitimate, free, online scholarship search websites.

Focus your efforts on those scholarships where you have the greatest chance of meeting the requirements. Your counselor can provide you with information on, and sometimes even nominate you for, scholarships offered by local groups and individuals. Define yourself and identify organizations looking to provide support for students like you, based on your religious affiliation, heritage and family employers, among other criteria. Once you've applied for scholarships, be on the lookout for responses or requests for any follow-up actions on your part. A **Scholarship Log** is provided to help you keep track of available scholarships and due dates, so you don't miss out on any opportunities.

"We have a scholarship consideration deadline of December 1, in advance of our regular decision deadline of January 2. All applicants should note this deadline if they want to be considered for scholarships."

—JENNIFER SANDOVAL-DANCS, Director of Admission, Claremont McKenna College

UNDERSTANDING YOUR FINANCIAL AID AWARD

You will receive financial aid letters from each of the schools offering you admission. These letters may arrive with your acceptance or shortly after. They may all look different from one another, often making it difficult to compare them.

In order to compare your net cost to attend, start with total cost of attendance (tuition and fees, room and board, personal expenses, books and supplies, and travel) and subtract all grants and scholarships. If you plan to borrow to finance your net cost to attend, it's essential to compare the terms of available loans.

Financial Aid Worksheet

SCHOOL NAME					
CSS/PROFILE					
Code					
Priority Filing Deadline					
Closing Deadline					
Date Sent					
COF					
Deadline					
Date Sent					
SCHOOL FORMS					
Deadline					
Date Sent					
ISFAA					
Deadline					
Date Sent					
OTHER FORM(S)					
Deadline					
Date Sent					
FINANCIAL AID CONTACT					
Name					
Telephone					
Email					

Financial Aid Worksheet

SCHOOL NAME					
CSS/PROFILE					
Code					
Priority Filing Deadline					
Closing Deadline					
Date Sent					
COF					
Deadline					
Date Sent					
SCHOOL FORMS					
Deadline					
Date Sent					
ISFAA					
Deadline					
Date Sent					
OTHER FORM(S)					
Deadline					
Date Sent					
FINANCIAL AID CONTACT					
Name					
Telephone					
Email					

Scholarship Log

Name of Scholarship	Due Date	Date Submitted

CHAPTER 7

THE HOME STRETCH: YOU'RE ALMOST DONE!

You have submitted your applications and you're almost done! It's an exciting and nervous time while you await decisions.

If you have any new positive developments relevant to your candidacy, reach out to admissions reps to make them aware. Be mindful to share only significant and meaningful accomplishments that you feel enhance your application. If you've received any special attention or recognition, you should let them know about it. For example, if you've won an award or contest or have had your work published, take pride and share your good news with your admissions reps. Athletic, artistic and musical accomplishments should also be shared. Informing Admissions of your achievements could have a positive impact on your application.

> "Students can always feel free to submit additional materials and updates to their file after completion. Students are welcome to continue to update their application, even after our deadline."
>
> —NICOLE KELMAN, Assistant Director of Admission, Muhlenberg College

Remember, colleges and universities typically request your final year grades, so don't let procrastination get the better of you. Your admission and financial aid offers are contingent on maintaining your academic standing. If you've had a change of heart about the schools you've applied to, it's not too late to add to your list. There's still time to apply to schools with both rolling and late admissions deadlines. Check with your counselor for a list of schools still accepting applications.

While it seems like your application process is coming to a close, here are a few more things you should do:

✓ Confirm that all your application materials have been received. It's your responsibility to make sure your admissions files are complete. There are so many different reasons students don't hear back from colleges and universities after submitting applications. Occasionally, the schools do not receive recommendations, transcripts or standardized test scores. Not all schools send correspondence requesting missing information.

✓ Follow up by phone, check the online service your school uses or consult the online tracking system many colleges and universities assign to applicants in order to confirm your materials have been received. In the end, it's your responsibility to ensure your applications are complete and that all the required

My daughter's friend submitted an application to a school that reviews them on a rolling basis, hoping to receive an early answer. Months passed until she learned her teacher recommendations had never been received, delaying review of her application.

components have been submitted and received by your schools.

✓ Use the **Application Checklist** worksheet you completed when you were submitting your applications for this follow-up step. As you go down the list and confirm receipt of each component, check "R" for received. Once you have completed this step of the process, your applications are done!

"The CMC Admission Office has an application portal where applicants can confirm the application credentials our office has received and what items are lacking. The portal lists required application materials only and will not indicate, for example, if we have received an art or an athletic supplement."

—JENNIFER SANDOVAL-DANCS, Director of Admission, Claremont McKenna College

"Most schools will alert you when your file is complete. If they do so in writing or by email, keep a record of these contacts. If you have not heard from a school, contact them and note the date/time of contact and the name of the person with whom you spoke."

—ALISON ALMASIAN, Director of Admissions, St. Lawrence University

As admissions decisions are released, fill in the **AM I IN?** worksheet to keep track of your outcomes. You may be sorting through acceptances, possibly rejections and perhaps you have even been placed on a waitlist or two. Make sure you understand your options.

ADMITTED

Congratulations on your good news! All your hard work has paid off and it's time to celebrate. If you've received more than one offer, use the **Should I / Shouldn't I?** worksheet on page 162 to help you make your decision. It's been many months since you began your search and application process; you now know so much more about yourself, your future goals, and higher education opportunities

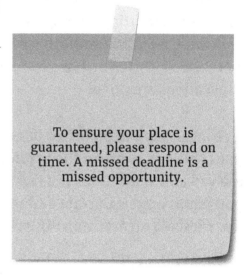

To ensure your place is guaranteed, please respond on time. A missed deadline is a missed opportunity.

than you did when you started. Take the time to make sure you're choosing the school that's best for you. If you're not sure, don't feel rushed; you have until May 1st to reply. But once you make a decision, submit your reply and deposit. Then, inform all the other schools you've been admitted to that you will not be attending, so that your spot may be offered to another student. Write a simple letter thanking the admissions office for their acceptance and letting them know that you've decided to enroll elsewhere.

> **"There is no greater feeling than receiving your first college acceptance letter. Celebrate your acceptance. You have worked your entire secondary education to achieve this success and regardless of what school the letter comes from, celebrate that milestone, because you only get ONE first college acceptance letter!"**
>
> **—KEVIN O'SULLIVAN, Director of Undergraduate Admissions, Manhattanville College**

WAITLISTED

Neither acceptance nor rejection, this outcome requires your immediate attention. If you've been waitlisted by one of your top-priority schools, the good news is you're still in the game. There are four things you should do immediately. First, send in the response card required to be included on the waitlist by the deadline, but preferably as soon as possible. You will not be placed on the list automatically. Second, contact your admissions rep by phone, email or handwritten note to express your continued interest in being admitted and to offer to provide any additional information in support of your candidacy. You may also want to refer back to your **Correspondence Journal** to reach out to contacts you made at the school earlier in the process. Update them about any new achievements not included in your file. If this is truly your top choice, let your admissions rep know that if you're admitted, you will definitely attend. Third, talk to your counselor and ask him or her to reach out to the school rep on your behalf, if they feel it's appropriate. Fourth, if you require financial aid, contact the school to ask whether aid will be available if you're admitted from the waitlist.

The number of students admitted from a waitlist varies by school and from year to year. While the admissions office may provide you with information about prior years' waitlists, there are no guarantees. You may be offered admission from a waitlist after deposits are due, so in the meantime, evaluate any other choices you may have and follow through with a decision and send in your deposit by the May 1st due date. Be aware, deposits are non-refundable, so if you're admitted from a waitlist and choose to attend that school, you'll forfeit the deposit you sent to the other school.

DELAYED ADMISSION

Some colleges and universities offer admission but not until the second semester or even the following fall. There are several things to think about if you're considering this option. Determine what you will do in the interim. Your choices will vary from school to school, depending on their policies. Your options may include participating in a special program, spending a semester abroad, attending another college or university, working, volunteering, or traveling. If you're thinking about spending the gap semester/year at another school, find out whether transfer credits will be accepted.

THE FINISH LINE

If you're considering more than one of your acceptances, look back at your *Getting Acquainted* worksheets from Chapter 4. If you visited a campus, try to remember how you felt while you were there. Locate all those brochures you collected and notes you took, and go back to websites and books you found helpful. Does one college or university have an academic program you are particularly interested in? Consider size, location, and distance from home, and campus personality. If financial aid is relevant, is the school's aid package adequate? Does one college or university have the Greek life or school spirit you are looking for? Do you feel like you belong as a member of the school community? Complete the **Should I / Shouldn't I?** worksheet provided in this chapter to help you organize your thoughts. Ask your parents for their input and seek your counselor's thoughts as well.

In the meantime, the schools you've already been admitted to may be reaching out to let you know about special programs and events for accepted students. Many colleges and universities host "admitted student" days, events held on campus that give you the opportunity to meet your future classmates, current students, faculty and administrators, and help you decide whether this is the community you'd like to be a part of. If you have the chance to attend, spend some time at the student center, read the notices posted by different clubs and organizations around campus and walk around the surrounding neighborhoods. Stop by the cafeteria and notice what students are doing— are they studying while eating or chatting and laughing? Talk to them. Do you feel like you belong?

> **"If a school meets the basic parameters of what you are looking for, go with your gut. If you step onto a campus and can see yourself there for the next four years don't discount that feeling in the final selection process."**
>
> **—ED CONNOR, Dean of Admissions, Worcester Polytechnic Institute**

Graduation is around the corner, but before all the big events and special celebrations begin, there are a few more items to check off your to-do list. Soon, you'll be a first year university student! But please ensure you've take care of the following, so no stumbling blocks land in your way:

- ✓ Many people have helped you throughout your search and application process. Thank your school counselor, recommendation writers and anyone else who has guided you along the way by writing them a note to express your appreciation for all their efforts. This is also a good opportunity to let your supporters know what your plans are for next fall.

- ✓ Although you may be tempted to trash your pile of admissions materials, don't. It's possible you will be asked to provide any or all of this information at different times throughout your college years when you apply for internships, jobs and any special academic programs. Sort through and save the following:

  - ✓ a final copy of each of your essays
  - ✓ a copy of your completed Common App, as your online account will become inactive soon
  - ✓ your test score report(s)
  - ✓ your transcript

- ✓ important school work, such as essays or research papers
- ✓ an updated list of activities and awards or honors to help you create your CV, when needed

✓ Accept the offer of admission from the college or university of your choice and submit your deposit by the May 1st deadline.

✓ Decline any other offers of admission to let the other schools know you will not be attending.

✓ Confirm that your secondary school has sent your final school report or transcript to your college or university.

✓ Apply for your student visa. Confirm what is required by checking with the admissions office.

✓ Finalize your financial aid details and follow up on any loose ends. Double-check that you've submitted all the required documents. If you have any questions or doubts, talk to your school counselor or call the financial aid office.

✓ Review your payment plan options and make sure your first payment is submitted on time.

✓ Get to know your future classmates on social media.

✓ Submit your housing choice, health forms, insurance documents and all other required forms on time.

✓ Complete any roommate surveys or requests.

✓ Register for any orientation programs offered.

✓ Complete your fall course registration by the required deadline.

✓ Complete any summer reading or pre-semester assignments.

✓ Get excited!

Am I In?

| SCHOOL NAME | ACCEPTED | | NOT ACCEPTED | DEFERRED | WAITLISTED | |
	RESPONSE/ DEPOSIT DEADLINE	DATE MAILED			RESPONSE DEADLINE	DATE RESPONDED

Should I / Shouldn't I?

School Name	What I Like	What I Don't Like	My Net Cost to Attend	Special Programs

Congratulations, we applaud your efforts!

Feel confident that you've submitted the best applications possible and optimized your chance for admission to the school that's best for you. You have so much to look forward to.

We wish you every success in university and beyond.

CHAPTER 8

THE INTERVIEWS

CONVERSATIONS WITH COLLEGE ADMISSIONS OFFICERS

While conducting research for *The University Bound Organizer* we were fortunate to have had the opportunity to interview many college admissions professionals. They were generous in sharing their many insights and experiences with us, and we are confident you will find these conversations invaluable.

Q. How essential is it to coordinate all schedules (standardized testing, college visits, application deadlines...)?

A. During the fall of your final year, demands run high and time is at a premium! Life doesn't stop for the college search and application process. It usually occurs in the context of extraordinarily busy lives marked by school studies, sports, extracurricular activities, and work. It is essential that students get in front of the process and streamline it wherever possible. Having a vision and a "plan of attack" will assist students in maintaining balance while achieving their ultimate goal: acceptance into college!

—LAURA A. BRUNO,
Associate Director of Admissions, York College,
The City University of New York

A. I often get asked about mistakes students make or common pitfalls in the process. My response is that students and families need to read the fine print, not assume anything! Even among similar institutions there will be different deadlines, requirements, etc. The process is full of institutional idiosyncrasies and students need to stay on top of it all. A master spreadsheet and/or schedule is essential to success.

—NANCY HARGRAVE MEISLAHN,
Dean of Admission and Financial Aid, Wesleyan University

Q. Which individual components must be in a student's file before you will begin to read the application?

A. Muhlenberg College requires all students to submit an online or paper Common Application, a personal essay, an official high school transcript, a guidance counselor recommendation, two high school teacher recommendations, official SAT and/or ACT scores, and the application fee.

Other non-required, yet highly recommended components are a campus visit and/or interview. If the student has chosen not to submit their SAT/ACT scores for review as a part of our SAT-optional policy, we require an interview with an Admissions Counselor and a graded paper from junior or senior year with the teacher's comments and grade, in lieu of scores.

—NICOLE KELMAN,
Assistant Director of Admission, Muhlenberg College

A. We only read complete applications—transcript, test scores, essay, teacher recommendation, and application fee.

—MARIA LAPINS,
Senior Assistant Director of Admission, University of Richmond

A. All of the required application materials must be in the applicant's file for the file to be flagged as complete and forwarded to the reader except the Midyear Report. We read applications without the Midyear Report. The required components of the freshmen application include: Common Application, Common Application Supplement including analytical essay, Secondary School Report with counselor letter, (2) Academic Teacher Evaluations, Official SAT or ACT scores (we do require the optional writing section of the ACT), Official High School Transcript.

—JENNIFER SANDOVAL-DANCS,
Director of Admission, Claremont McKenna College

Q. When you read an application, what grabs your attention?

A. Since St. Lawrence practices holistic review, I am looking at multiple elements of the application. In terms of the transcript, I am looking to see that the student has challenged him/ herself as much as possible within the context of the school's curriculum. I am also looking for evidence of intellectual curiosity, which is often noted in the recommendations from counselors and teachers. However, the item that most often grabs my attention is a well-written essay, which conveys something about the candidate that I might not realize from other parts of the student's file. This is where the candidate can distinguish him/herself as a unique individual.

—ALISON ALMASIAN,
Director of Admissions, St. Lawrence University

A. Attention to detail! It is evident when a student spent time on an application by using complete sentences to explain extracurricular activities and grammatical errors have been proofed in the essay.

—ANDREA BUCHANAN
Senior Assistant Director of Admissions, Coordinator for International Student Admissions, Gettysburg College

A. Every student has a story, so I look for the narrative elements in every document. I can usually find it in essays, even short essays, but there's also a four-year story in the transcript and often, good stories in letters of recommendation. I find that knowing something about how a student has changed over time gives me a much better fix on why Rochester would be a great next chapter for him or her.

—JONATHAN BURDICK,
Dean of Admissions and Financial Aid, University of Rochester

A. All schools are looking for the killer scores and top grades. Don't get me wrong, we like them too! That being said, how someone strikes balance in their lives, and the interesting ways in which they get involved outside of the classroom, are what catch my attention. These activities certainly demonstrate that they are an interesting person, and likely to get involved on our campus, but they also show that they are likely to have some balance in their lives and already possess some solid time management skills, which can be critical to success in college.

—ED CONNOR,
Dean of Admissions, Worcester Polytechnic University

A. Essays get my attention since they tell me quite a bit about the applicants.

—MUSA KHALIDI
Executive Director International Admissions, St. Lawrence University

A. When reading an application, the primary credential that grabs my attention is the student's transcript. The transcript tells the academic story of the student's four-year performance and oftentimes is the best indicator of the student's ability to be successful at the collegiate level. In addition to looking at the overall performance, I want to see how the student challenged themself at the high school level. Did the student challenge themself with a nice selection of honors and AP courses if their grades indicate that they were capable of performing well in the course? Next, I analyze the standardized test scores if the student chose to submit them. Were the scores consistent with the student's academic performance throughout high school? I also consider the student's IQ (*Interaction Quotient*) or demonstrated Interest. Has the student demonstrated a desire to be a part of the Manhattanville Community? Did they visit us at a High School Visit or College Fair? Have they visited the campus for a tour or Open House? Did the student interview with a member of our staff? One of my goals as an Admissions Director is to identify students who desire to be a member of the Manhattanville Community. I want Manhattanville to be a first choice school for the students who are applying to the College. In addition, we look at the recommendation letters and college essay.

—KEVIN O'SULLIVAN,
Director of Undergraduate Admissions, Manhattanville College

A. First and foremost, we try to determine if an applicant can succeed academically in our liberal arts curriculum. To that end, we are looking at the student's grades, specifically in his or her "academic" courses, which include math, science, English, history, and foreign language. These subjects are cornerstones of the curriculum here at Marymount, so we want to be sure that each incoming student has a strong foundation in them. Secondly, we are looking at students' SAT or ACT scores for further insight into their level of academic preparedness. Students who demonstrate strong grades and test scores are further rewarded with academic scholarships and admission to our College Honors Program.

A well-written essay also grabs my attention. The essay is your opportunity to show us (not tell us) something about yourself that is not apparent in the rest of your application. You can also show us, by carefully proofreading and editing your essay, that you are taking your Marymount application seriously.

It also catches my attention when a student understands and embodies Marymount's core values. Take the time to learn about the community you are applying to join. The successful Marymount student demonstrates independence, creativity, and ambition. I notice when a student has demonstrated these qualities in his or her previous school setting, by joining clubs, taking on leadership roles, or even speaking up in class. These qualities can shine through in your activities lists, essay, or recommendations.

—JIM ROGERS,
Dean of Admission, Marymount Manhattan College

A. Transcript, SAT Scores, Teacher and Counselor Recommendation, Essay, Extracurricular Activities, Financial Aid: Is the student applying for aid? Be sure to check yes if your family is interested in receiving aid or merit scholarships.

—ZEE SANTIAGO,
Assistant Director of Admissions, Trinity College

Q. Do you welcome email or telephone follow-up questions from applicants? Do you have a preference?

A. Absolutely! Applicants are always welcome to contact the Office of Admissions with questions or concerns. I strongly encourage students to be proactive about the process. While either a telephone call or an email are acceptable, I find email to be slightly more preferable because it creates a history and a record of applicants' inquiries for future reference.

—LAURA A. BRUNO,
Associate Director of Admissions, York College,
The City University of New York

A. Email and telephone conversations are welcome for genuine questions or clarification. Calling to check to see if all the application documents have been received can be tedious, especially when students can mostly check online now. If there is a discrepancy, please do reach out. If there's a significant accomplishment or update, please do reach out to let us know. But many of us are receiving hundreds of emails a day and clutter isn't necessary.

—ANDREA BUCHANAN
Assistant Director of Admissions, Coordinator for International Student
Admissions, Gettysburg College

A. I welcome questions from all applicants at all times. E-mail tends to be the best means of communication since it allows us to look up records before answering questions.

—MUSA KHALIDI
Executive Director International Admissions, St. Lawrence University

A. Definitely. We have four freshman Admission Counselors, two Transfer Admission Counselors, and a Director of International Recruitment who are available to answer questions at any point in the process. (A complete list of Admission representatives and their contact information can be found at www.mmm.edu/become/meet.html.) We welcome questions by either email or telephone, depending on what works best for you. Since high school students tend to be in school during regular business hours, many students find email to be a more practical way of reaching their counselors.

Just keep in mind that, just as you have the option of contacting us via phone or email, our counselors will be trying to reach you through both media as well. Be sure to check your email and voicemail regularly for important messages throughout the application process.

Lastly, I encourage all applicants to take the initiative to contact our office directly, rather than delegating that task to a parent or other family member. It can be tempting to let a parent sit in the driver's seat, especially because you are often very busy in school and because the application process is so overwhelming. While we do appreciate connecting with parents, we always prefer speaking to the student directly. So do not be afraid to reach out to us—we notice and appreciate the gesture.

—JIM ROGERS,
Dean of Admission, Marymount Manhattan College

A. Yes, either is sufficient and an effective way to maintain a relationship with the institution of choice. No, I am accessible either way.

—ZEE SANTIAGO,
Assistant Director of Admissions, Trinity College

Q. Are thank-you letters to Admissions staff and faculty appreciated and noted?

A. Thank-you letters are always appreciated; however, they do not impact the Admission decision.

—LAURA A. BRUNO,
Associate Director of Admissions, York College,
The City University of New York

A. Yes! Even at a small school like Marymount, we receive thousands of applications every year. We keep track of all correspondence with students, including thank-you notes, emails, phone calls, visits to the school, and even posts on our Facebook page. By sending a thank-you note, you are demonstrating your organization and interest in Marymount. That conscientiousness does not go unnoticed.

—JIM ROGERS,
Dean of Admission, Marymount Manhattan College

A. Yes, it is greatly appreciated! Aim to maintain consistent communication with the colleges and universities of your choice. Build a relationship with the admissions officer that travels to your region. Set up interviews if possible. Speak with the representative at a fair or when they visit your high school; take their business card, and follow up. Visit, take a tour, and sit in on an information session. Attend Open Houses if they are available. If you cannot visit (i.e., distance), ask for an alumni interview.

—ZEE SANTIAGO,
Assistant Director of Admissions, Trinity College

Q. Do you recommend applicants who have demonstrated a significant commitment to a co-curricular or extracurricular activity support their activities with supplemental materials (i.e., CV/resume, portfolio)?

A. We strongly recommend that applicants follow our application format and complete both the Common Application and the NYU Supplement in their entirety. Students should detail their extracurricular accomplishments on the application, and not expect that we will review a resume instead. For students who are applying to a creative arts program, we do have very specific instructions with regard to the submission of portfolios.

—SHAWN ABBOTT,
Assistant Vice President for Admissions, New York University

A. Resumes (CVs) are common and should probably go in an application unless the school instructs you not to send one. Keep it to one page; longer resumes look silly—even lazy in a sense, because it doesn't tell us that you've learned how to focus your time and set priorities. I don't think including extra materials ever hurts an application, but I wouldn't encourage a student to spend too much time or put too much stock into this approach unless you're applying for an art, music, etc., major. It's hit-or-miss whether the admissions readers are going to review it, much less appreciate it. Increasingly reading is online, so embedding a link to a webpage with your art or a *brief* video clip of a performance can be effective.

—JONATHAN BURDICK,
Dean of Admissions and Financial Aid, University of Rochester

Q. If a student submits additional supplemental materials in support of his or her application that are not in accordance with your submission requirements, will that material still be considered?

A. The reality is that we do expect students to follow our application instructions with great detail. When an applicant fails to do this—and insists on sending us material not requested— it can potentially damage the impression our readers have of the candidate. We explicitly ask that students refrain from submitting supplementary materials outside of those that are required for our arts programs. Students who ignore this direction can be at a competitive disadvantage in the admission process.

—SHAWN ABBOTT,
Assistant Vice President for Admissions, New York University

A. CV and resumes are great if more explanation for the activities is needed. If the resume is just a listing of activities and no explanation, then it is just another piece of paper to look at. If a school does not ask for a portfolio, it is not necessary to send one. Often times, we do not have the ability to load it into the file if it isn't required.

—ANDREA BUCHANAN
Senior Assistant Director of Admissions,
Coordinator for International Student Admissions, Gettysburg College

A. Overall, I'd say go for it—send it and hope for the best. Yes, you have to allow for the possibility that a college admission office will choose to judge you for not following their rules. However, if the place isn't going to take the time to appreciate who you really are, maybe that's not where you belong anyway.

—JONATHAN BURDICK,
Dean of Admissions and Financial Aid, University of Rochester

A. Students (preferably students, not parents) should always contact admissions offices to see what is appropriate; sending too much of what we do not want may be viewed as a lack of ability to follow directions. If the material is not something an office considers, then in many cases it may be disregarded. Call each college/university to which you plan to apply.

—DARRYL W. JONES,
Senior Associate Director of Admissions, Gettysburg College

A. Yes I do since we are an institution that puts heavy emphasis on holistic review. Students should always submit material which they believe will make them stand out.

—MUSA KHALIDI
Executive Director International Admissions, St. Lawrence University

Q. Do you often note discrepancies in information between the Common Application and supplemental information submitted? If yes, can you elaborate?

A. Discrepancies of any major type are not common; when we encounter them, we often call college counselors and contact the applicant to get clarity. Honest mistakes are not a problem!

—DARRYL W. JONES,
Senior Associate Director of Admissions, Gettysburg College

A. Discrepancies can come in many different forms. One can be with a student who indicates a very high interest in a club or organization but fails to elaborate on it when submitting other pieces of information. Others can be declaring an interest to be a part of a learning disabilities program and then not going into a bit more detail about how and to what depth they may need services. Other discrepancies may seem minimal but actually cause mass chaos. This can be that addresses, DOB, or SSN do not match what is on a high school transcript.

—SUNIL SAMUEL,
Director of Admission, Hofstra University

Q. Who is responsible for confirming a student's admission file is complete? Does your Admission Office have an online system for students to check whether their standardized scores have been received? If so, are the submitted scores logged in by test date so that students can confirm that all sent scores have been received?

A. The admissions office is responsible for confirming a file is complete and we are always directly in touch with students if a necessary document is missing from the file. We will not review a file if it is incomplete. We will reach out past the due date to get information that we need.

—ANDREA BUCHANAN
Senior Assistant Director of Admissions, Coordinator for International
Student Admissions, Gettysburg College

A. An application specialist who works closely with me.

—MUSA KHALIDI
Executive Director International Admissions, St. Lawrence University

A. The student is solely responsible for confirming their admission file is complete. Muhlenberg College provides every applicant with an identification number and password to check the status of their application online through an ePortal account that the student can create. This account will show the student which credentials we have received and what is still missing. We highly encourage every student to frequently check their status throughout the application process. If the student is unsure if we have received a credential, we encourage the student to contact our office by phone. Many times students think we have received all components because they were mailed to our office, but students should always follow up by checking online or calling our office. Once an application becomes complete, our office will mail a postcard to the student stating that their file is complete and ready for review. Students can always feel free to submit additional materials and updates to their file after completion.

—NICOLE KELMAN,
Assistant Director of Admission, Muhlenberg College

A. We have a staff of six people who track applications, additionally each officer checks all the pieces within an application when he/she opens the file.

—MARIA LAPINS,
Senior Assistant Director of Admission, University of Richmond

A. The CMC Admission Office has an application portal where applicants can confirm the application credentials our office has received and what items are lacking. The portal lists required application materials only and will not indicate, for example, if we have received an art or an athletic supplement. Our application portal simply indicates we have received standardized scores for the applicant, so the only way for an applicant to confirm we received all tests they have requested is to contact our office directly.

—JENNIFER SANDOVAL-DANCS,
Director of Admission, Claremont McKenna College

Q. Once the application deadline has arrived, will you notify candidates of any missing components from their file? Will you allow the students to provide that information at any time past the due date?

A. Muhlenberg will not notify a candidate of any missing components from their file, especially after the deadline has passed. We have very late deadlines for both Regular and Early Decision, so students have ample time to make sure we have received their required components for admission, and we encourage students to check their status online at our admissions ePortal. Students are welcome to continue to update their application, even after our deadline.

—NICOLE KELMAN,
Assistant Director of Admission, Muhlenberg College

A. We notify via BannerWeb. Once a student applies, he/she is given a user name and password to check if credentials are here. We also send emails and letters when the application is incomplete.

—MARIA LAPINS,
Senior Assistant Director of Admission, Richmond University

A. CMC does not typically notify applicants of missing application credentials. We count on the application portal to convey such information to the applicant. We do send out a missing letter and email to applicants in early March if the application is lacking required material.

—JENNIFER SANDOVAL-DANCS,
Director of Admission, Claremont McKenna College

Q. Do applications get lost because they are addressed incorrectly so that the material does not find its way to the Admissions Office properly?

A. If something is not addressed correctly but goes to another area of the university there is a high likelihood that it will get back to us, but there are no guarantees. Since many students are applying online these days and more and more is being done to transmit letters of recommendation, a transcript, etc., electronically, less and less is being lost. This has never been a problem that we have encountered, even though we have an extremely high application volume.

—SUNIL SAMUEL,
Director of Admission, Hofstra University

Q. When reviewing an application are you influenced by any of the following: misspellings, typographical errors, sloppy presentation?

A. Very much so. Paying attention to details is a very important part of the application process.

—MUSA KHALIDI
Executive Director International Admissions, St. Lawrence University

A. Yes!

—ANDREA BUCHANAN
Senior Assistant Director of Admissions, Coordinator for International Student Admissions, Gettysburg College

A. Many of these issues are not deal breakers, but they may influence the decision process when we assess the students' desirability to attend. If we run into these errors we question if the students are really serious about attending our institution. Misspellings and typos are very bothersome during the essay evaluation and may affect the readers' motivation to continue with reading the essay.

—SUNIL SAMUEL,
Director of Admission, Hofstra University

Q. Are there application missteps you observe repeatedly that you would like to caution future applicants about?

A. Yes! In no particular order...

Think about what your email address may or may not say about you.

Make sure that you are regularly checking the email address you provided to schools. They will be sending important information through that medium.

The correct term is "honor roll," not "honor role."

Have at least two other people read your essay before submitting it. You want to make sure that you are conveying the message you intended as well as make sure that any errors have been corrected. It is extremely difficult to proofread your own work.

Make sure that you have confirmation that your applications are complete. Most schools will alert you when your file is complete. If they do so in writing or by email, keep a record of these contacts. If you have not heard from a school, contact them and then note the date/time of contact and the name of the person with whom you spoke.

—ALISON ALMASIAN,
Director of Admissions, St. Lawrence University

A. Double check that your essay is for the right school/application.

—ANDREA BUCHANAN
Senior Assistant Director of Admissions, Coordinator for International
Student Admissions, Gettysburg College

A. I often joke with families that if you were to graph careless essay and application errors against the time of submission you'd see the errors peak around 2 a.m....if it is that late, put it down and take a fresh look at it in the morning. I know everyone is busy, but the application and essay are reflections on you as an individual, and you shouldn't wait to the last minute to complete them. Give the process adequate time. Ask someone to review the application and essay for you. Make sure you are comfortable with them before hitting submit!

—ED CONNOR,
Dean of Admissions, Worcester Polytechnic University

A. Students should avoid relying on spell-check and auto fill-in for essays and supplements. The supplement for Lafayette College should not mention Lehigh University; the act of joining an honors society is an "induction," not an "abduction"...usually proofreading remedies that though. Students should avoid using essay "banks" for ideas—we scan those to know what the essays are, and plagiarism is something we do not take lightly.

—DARRYL W. JONES,
Senior Associate Director of Admissions, Gettysburg College

A. Our admissions office will often receive phone calls from applicants who say they were unaware that their file was incomplete. It is the student's responsibility to make sure their file is complete. I would also tell students how important it is to demonstrate interest in the college they are applying to, especially if that school is a top choice. Muhlenberg wants to accept students who want to be at Muhlenberg. We will document if a student has interacted with our staff directly through email conversations, phone conversations, campus tours, information sessions, and personal interviews with a staff member. Students should be proactive and take charge. We encourage students to take control of their own college process instead of a parent leading the search. We would love to meet all our applicants in person, if possible.

—NICOLE KELMAN,
Assistant Director of Admission, Muhlenberg College

A. The most common misstep I routinely observe is when a student writes to me and mentions a different college name. Also, students sometimes write and and ask me about a major that does not exist on my campus.

—MUSA KHALIDI
Executive Director International Admissions, St. Lawrence University

A. This is your process—take ownership and follow up with your colleges. Pay attention to deadlines.

—MARIA LAPINS,
Senior Assistant Director of Admission, University of Richmond

A. Obviously with the emergence of new technology and advanced "spell check" features, I have noticed an increase in the number of essays that contain some type of error. If you are going to send the same essay to every college, you should at the very least proofread what you send. Every year, there are dozens and dozens of students who write an essay about how much they love Manhattanville College, but then at some point within the essay have a different college's name inserted into the essay!

Oftentimes, I feel as though students feel a need to sign up for twenty different clubs just to show that they were "involved" with a large number of activities in high school. In reality, what I look for when evaluating an applicant is passion. Be passionate about the activities you take part in. You don't need to do a little bit of everything. Rather, put everything into the areas about which you are passionate. As a Director, I try to attract and enroll students who can enhance the College environment. I don't want students who have just a little interest in a lot of areas, it creates a bland environment. I want students who have passion for what they do and want to bring that passion to the College.

—KEVIN O'SULLIVAN,
Director of Undergraduate Admissions, Manhattanville College

A. There are many missteps that can slow down the process, but here are a few:

1. If you are applying electronically, please inform your guidance counselor so they can forward the appropriate high school information.

2. Do not throw a school off your list just because the price may seem out of your range. You do not know what their scholarship structure is.

3. Visit, visit, visit.

4. Be very aware of the application deadlines when researching schools.

5. Ask questions all the time.

—SUNIL SAMUEL,
Director of Admission, Hofstra University

A. We have a scholarship consideration deadline of December 1, in advance of our regular decision deadline of January 2. All applicants should note this deadline if they want to be considered for scholarships. The only additional thing they need to do is indicate "yes" on the Common Application when asked if they want to be considered for merit scholarships. Many times we are contacted by admitted students in April inquiring about scholarships.

Applicants should not hesitate to contact the admission office to confirm we have received their application if they have heard nothing from us and it has been *two weeks* since submitting their application. We send an acknowledgment within two weeks of our receipt of the application to the applicant via email, and we also provide the applicant application portal instructions. Each year there are a handful of applicants who contact our office in April inquiring about their decision and we never received their application.

We require standardized test scores from the College Board or ACT testing agency; we do not accept scores from the high school transcript or self-reported scores.

CMC requires both a personal statement that is part of the Common Application and an analytical essay, which is part of the CMC Supplement; these essays should be different both in writing style and in the content of the essay. Some essays sound very similar and this does not assist us in understanding their different writing styles and viewpoints. If the essays sound too similar they are essentially limiting what we learn from them if they are covering similar topics in both essays.

We require the Common Application and Supplement in order for an application to be complete. There are applicants who submit one without the other, and we cannot access the application from the Common Application unless both applications have been submitted online. If an applicant chooses to mail the application, then both the applications must be mailed.

—JENNIFER SANDOVAL-DANCS,
Director of Admission, Claremont McKenna College

Q. Are there additional comments or anecdotes you would like to share?

A. There is an old saying in college admissions: "The thicker the file, the thicker the student." More is rarely better. Applicants should be effective ambassadors for themselves and must remember their audience: admission counselors are often expected to read between 1,000 and 3,000 applications each year. No admission counselor can read that many applications well if each of those applicants follows his or her own format and submits a bucket of supplementary materials.

—SHAWN ABBOTT,
Assistant Vice President for Admissions, New York University

A. Admissions staff and counselors talk often of the importance of "fit." Each college has a distinct personality, as do the applicants. It is important for students to understand themselves and know what they are seeking from their college experience. Similarly, colleges will seek evidence that an applicant will contribute to their unique community. Both colleges and students have a duty to communicate who they are as effectively as possible to ensure the best possible matches.

—ALISON ALMASIAN,
Director of Admissions, St. Lawrence University

A. Getting organized and staying organized are certainly two of the biggest tasks that high school students face during the process of applying to college. While parents and counselors can assist, the ultimate asset in the college admissions process is a carefully orchestrated plan.

Keeping tabs on letters and emails, tracking deadlines, and scheduling tasks is essential for success. After all, a missed deadline, a forgotten application fee, or a late essay submission can be the difference between a fat acceptance packet and the dreaded rejection letter. Organization maximizes success while minimizing the stress associated with the college application process.

—LAURA A. BRUNO,
Associate Director of Admissions, York College, The City University of New York

A. For the colleges you really want to go to, consider everything listed as "optional" in admissions is actually "mandatory." That's SAT Subject Exams, extra letters of recommendation, invitations to apply for special scholarships or programs, interviews, events in your area, etc. If you literally *can't* complete that extra form or *can't* attend, you can't—but don't *choose* to ignore any opportunity the college admissions office says may be valuable.

It's a fine idea to have an email address that's just for college applications, but if you do, check that email. I see hundreds of high school seniors missing opportunities because they're not in the regular email habit. If one in-box eventually gets too cluttered with email from colleges you've stopped considering, start a new email address and resend that to the smaller number of colleges that are still on your list.

Nothing replaces a campus visit, so seize any opportunity that comes your way to look at college campuses.

The supplements on Common App often mean more to the school's readers than the initial Common App document itself. If you rewrite your main personal statement ten times, don't blow it by submitting a supplement with brief, error-prone, weak short answers on the supplements.

With admissions and aid counselors, after an interview, visit, etc., handwritten thank-you notes work well. Yet this advantage that is relatively easy to gain is often ignored.

—JONATHAN BURDICK,
Dean of Admissions and Financial Aid, University of Rochester

A. The application process can be very stressful and riddled with anxiety-provoking moments, but try and have fun. Visit schools. Get a feel for what they can offer you. In the end, four years goes very quickly when you find the right match, but can go much more slowly if you choose a school for the wrong reasons. If a school meets the basic parameters of what you are looking for, go with your gut. If you step onto a campus and can see yourself there for the next four years, don't discount that feeling in the final selection process. And last but not least, communicate with your parents. You don't want to find out at the eleventh hour that you are on a completely different page than they are!

—ED CONNOR,
Dean of Admissions, Worcester Polytechnic University

A. The admissions process is human, and we look for reasons to admit students, not to deny them. As simple as it may seem, if you are genuine, you always enhance your chances to be admitted if you are academically competitive.

Some things to remember:

1. At a given college or university, there are far more academically competitive applicants than there are places in the entering class, so representing all that you do beyond academics with authenticity is very important.

2. Representing yourself honestly rather than "marketing yourself" will help you to stand out, because too many students try to use the same "devices" based on what they've heard "works" to get admitted.

3. Ask admissions professionals for advice—we enjoy sharing it!

4. Remember to be a student who is an applicant, not an applicant who is a student— you'll enjoy the process more.

—DARRYL W. JONES,
Senior Associate Director of Admissions, Gettysburg College

A. My favorite part about working in college admissions is helping a student and their family through the entire college process from beginning to end, and finding the right match. I know when I meet a great student that is a perfect fit for Muhlenberg. When a student realizes that Muhlenberg is a perfect fit for them in return, that is the best feeling. Seeing that student arrive on campus, flourish as an individual, and graduate is the ultimate goal. My job is to create a bond with a student and help them through the complicated college admissions journey. I also enjoy keeping in contact with students once they arrive and making sure they are receiving the experience on campus they expected. I always hope to convey in words how extraordinary my college experience was at Muhlenberg so that another student will have the opportunity to experience the same.

—NICOLE KELMAN,
Assistant Director of Admission, Muhlenberg College

A. I would like to say that students should always look for the right fit college and not be influenced only by the big name or the rank. Further, both applicants and admissions officers are partners in this endeavor and we have the same goal: student success. I wish all students the very best!!

—MUSA KHALIDI,
Executive Director International Admissions, St. Lawrence University

A. My biggest piece of advice to navigating the college search and application process is to take a deep breath! You will often hear through the various forms of media as well as from colleges and high schools about the ultra-competitive admissions standards. However, if you conduct your proper research to find out the academic profiles and requirements of the colleges you are interested in, heed the advice of your school counselors, and take the time to visit the colleges that you are considering, you will most likely find that after the application and admissions process is complete, you will be happy with the results. If you are honest with yourself and honest with the process, you will most likely find out that you end up at the college where you belong! Keep in mind that there are thousands of colleges throughout the United States and a majority of the colleges admit more than 50 percent of the applicants to their college!

One last piece of advice, especially for parents! Be sure to celebrate your (or your son's or daughter's) successes! There is no greater feeling than receiving your first college acceptance letter. In many cases, your first acceptance letter may not be from your first choice college, and that's OK! Celebrate your acceptance. You have worked your entire secondary education to achieve this success and regardless of what school the letter comes from, celebrate that milestone, because you only get ONE first college acceptance letter!

—KEVIN O'SULLIVAN,
Director of Undergraduate Admissions, Manhattanville College

A. The majority of our applicants do a great job of submitting all of the application materials by the deadline, so it can be done. Please do not hesitate to contact the admission office if you do have questions. We would rather handle the questions upfront than deal with them later in the process when it can be more difficult to resolve the problem.

—JENNIFER SANDOVAL-DANCS,
Director of Admission, Claremont McKenna College

CONVERSATIONS ABOUT FINANCIAL AID

Several years ago, we had the opportunity to attend a financial aid seminar featuring Jacquelyn Nealon, Ed.D., Vice President of Enrollment, Communications and Marketing at New York Institute of Technology. We left the presentation with a better understanding of the financial aid process and greater confidence that it could be successfully conquered. We were thrilled when Dr. Nealon agreed to speak with us about financial aid.

Q. When discussing the early stages of the college process, you made a profound statement, "everybody can afford to go to college." Can we quote you?

A. Absolutely. I feel 100 percent confident when I look a prospective college student directly in the eye and say, "If you want to go to college this fall, you absolutely can afford to go to college!" The key is for students to stay open-minded about the thousands of colleges and universities that exist in the United States today; ranging from elite, high-priced private institutions to larger, public, low-priced community colleges. There isn't just one college out there for each student. There are hundreds. So every student can get admitted to college and every student can afford to go to college.

Q. What is the most common mistake you see when students apply for financial aid?

A. Missing deadlines, failing to follow through when asked for additional information, and starting the process too late are the most common mistakes that students make when applying for financial aid. The key is to apply as early as possible, stay ahead of deadlines, respond quickly, and not be afraid to ask questions when you are not sure about the process or information you have received.

Q. Do you have an anecdote you would like to add?

A. Over the years, I have counseled hundreds and hundreds of students and their families about how to apply for financial aid, how to choose a college that makes not only good academic sense but also good financial sense, and how to make informed choices. These students have worked so hard for eighteen years to build up to this very exciting time in their lives. Their parents have been dreaming of sending their child off to college since the moment the child was born. Their hopes are high, the stakes seem high, and the fear can be debilitating. One of the scariest conversations a parent can think about having with their child is, "I'm so proud of you. You were admitted to all of these terrific schools. But I can't afford to send you to the one you chose."

I like to remind students and their parents to take a deep breath, take a moment to appreciate the amazing accomplishments that have led to this point, compliment the students for committing to continuing their educations by attending college, and then repeat after me: "Where the student goes to college is less significant than the fact that the student

GOES TO COLLEGE. The most important factor over a lifetime is having the tools of a college education in your tool belt and knowing how to use them to create a successful career."

CONVERSATIONS WITH SECONDARY SCHOOL PROFESSIONALS

Secondary/high school professionals are the front-line advisors. They possess a wealth of information and expertise on the college admissions process.

Q. Please comment on the importance of utilizing the resources of the school guidance department for students and their parents.

A. The School Guidance department has a wealth of information for the students and the families. College Admissions representatives often make an outreach to the local high schools for the area they are responsible for reading. These representatives value the relationships developed between the high school counselor and their students. Each year these reps either visit the schools and meet with prospective students and counselors or communicate with them at local venues, over the phone, or through email. The HS Guidance departments are typically the first to be aware of any changes in admission requirements or information that would be relevant to any prospective student.

Additionally, HS counselors work very closely with the actual college applications that students complete—they are an extremely valuable resource when unsure how to proceed with a particular application. Use their expertise—they see hundreds of applications and essays and will be able to offer valuable insight into your responses. This is also true for your student resume and college essays. While we always recommend an English teacher review the essays for grammar, the counselors understand what colleges are looking for with respect to the personal statements and the individual supplements. Again, they see hundreds of essays and have worked with very successful students—please utilize their expertise!

It is imperative that students develop the relationship with their high school counselor.

The student-counselor relationship is critical on so many levels. Counselors are first and foremost trained to assist with many particular areas related to stress, time management, and crisis intervention. Additionally, high school counselors have a specialization in college admissions and the college application process. When students enter ninth grade (secondary school) they often become overwhelmed with the stress of their transcript, standardized testing, and college level courses. Students must reach out to the counselor for guidance! As this relationship is cultivated, the counselor is able to assist in carving the path that their students will follow with respect to courses, activities, community service, summer experiences, and finally college selections.

—REBECCA GOTTESMAN,
Assistant Principal, Locust Valley High School

A. It's impossible for any college counselor to know everything about all colleges, but they are great resources for helping families conduct their research and for thinking about the process.

—NANETTE TARBOUNI,
Director, College Counseling, John Burroughs School

Q. Given the fixed number of standardized test dates, how do you guide your students in establishing a schedule and keeping track of this schedule?

A. In our Parent/Student Handbook for Upper School families, we print the list of dates for the ACT and the SAT/SAT Subject Tests for the year for all families to view.

We also have the dates listed on the school's master calendar.

In the early fall of junior year, all parents and students receive a calendar of "Important Dates" for the year that includes our recommendations for test registration for both the ACT and SAT.

As we begin individual meetings with juniors in the winter, we review each student's plan for testing and reaffirm those choices in a "wrap-up" letter that we send to the student along with their initial college list.

Over the summer, we send letters to seniors (last year students) reminding them of upcoming test dates for the fall.

—AMY BAUMGARTEL SINGER,
Director of College Counseling, The Wheeler School

Q. How do you suggest students get organized and prepare to complete the Common Application?

A. I ask students to write down all the things they spend time doing outside of their academic classes, homework, and sleeping. All of it helps tell the story of who they are and what they might bring to a college community. Once they get this global view of how they spend their time, they can begin to decide which activities carry the greatest importance in their lives and what they want to include on the Common App.

The piece of the Common App that obviously requires the most thought is the personal statement. I like to pose the following question to students as they ponder their topics: "When the admissions committee is sitting at the table choosing between you and other students with the same grades and SAT scores, what do you want them to say about you?" Indeed it is a daunting concept for the average seventeen-year-old, but forcing them to introspectively consider what is genuinely unique about themselves and what they consider most important for the committee to know is a great exercise. Pragmatically, it also tends to produce the most human, honest, and individualized pieces of writing.

As an exercise, I ask students to write a letter of recommendation for themselves from the perspective of the college counselor. "What would you say?" This is a great essay "brainstormer" and it can be helpful later when writing the counselor letter of reference in understanding what the student values most about his or her accomplishments.

—PAUL W. HORGAN,
Director of College Counseling, Cape Henry Collegiate School

Q. A student's resume/CV is a snapshot of his or her secondary school years. Can you tell us how the student can use this resume/CV to highlight his or her accomplishments?

A. Our students are encouraged to put together their resumes through the resume builder function in the Naviance system or use the templates that we share with them in our College Counseling Handbook, which they receive in January of their junior year. However, we do not encourage students to submit these resumes to colleges (unless it is an athletic or special talent CV that a coach or professor might need to see). Students are often asked to report their activities in a particular format prescribed by the colleges themselves. Many colleges permit the use of the Common Application. To help our students prepare for this request we give our juniors a sample of the activities section on the Common Application and ask them to complete that as a rough draft. It is reviewed with their counselor for completeness and then used as a source document for the completion of the actual applications, both the Common Application and other applications, in the fall of their senior year.

—AMY BAUMGARTEL SINGER,
Director of College Counseling, The Wheeler School

A. The CV is exactly that—a way to highlight students' accomplishments! Emphasize students' strengths and leadership first and foremost. Every student has a unique set of strengths and the CV should highlight those as applicable. For example, a strong athlete must highlight all athletic achievements, awards, and leadership first and foremost. Students with research accolades should begin with those. Every CV must be unique to the students' accomplishments.

Make sure you don't overlook the small stuff! Nothing is irrelevant, everything counts!

—REBECCA GOTTESMAN,
Assistant Principal, Locust Valley High School

A. Remember that colleges are not looking for CVs that are a "mile wide and an inch deep." Students should consider highlighting the things into which they have poured the most time and effort, finding the things that have meant the most to them and the things in which they have made the greatest impact. The Common App and most other applications have space for students to fill in their activities. Students should remember to list these *"in their order of importance to you"* as the directions indicate. Students need to understand that college admissions officers are trying to get a sense of the individual by evaluating how that individual has spent his or her time. Being an avid skier or rock climber may tell as much and count as much as listing that you fulfilled twenty hours of a community service requirement at the local shelter.

Students should remember to explain their activities if they are not commonly understood things. For example, in Virginia Beach, the annual Neptune Festival selects a court of "Neptune Princesses" from a competitive group of local teens. In reality, this is quite an honor and it carries with it serious community service investment and a year-long commitment. Without the explanation, an admissions reader could misinterpret it as "fluff." At the nearby Suffolk Peanut Festival, they crown a "Peanut Princess!" You get the drift. Explain, explain, explain. But don't be so wordy that it is cumbersome.

—PAUL W. HORGAN,
Director of College Counseling, Cape Henry Collegiate School

Q. The application process does not end once the student submits his or her application. What do you advise the student to do from this point on?

A. Read your email! Colleges communicate primarily through email and expect timely responses. Failure to respond may result in missed opportunities (scholarships, housing, registration for courses). Many times colleges email students an access code or special link for the purpose of tracking their application materials. BE SURE TO CHECK THESE LINKS FREQUENTLY!

One way to stay organized is to keep a list of the schools you applied to next to your computer with each school's user name and password. The user name and password always vary based on the school and it is best to be able to easily access this information. Students often become frustrated when they forget this information and that only delays this process.

Please continue to update your HS counselor. The counselors are often aware of new and additional opportunities that become available. The more you stay in touch with your counselor, the more opportunities you will have. In addition, counselors are often in contact with college representatives and are always happy to provide follow-up information to the colleges their students have applied to.

Most important, if students are deferred or offered a spot on the waitlist, the counselor is the best advocate you have and will reach out to the representative from that particular school to continue to support their student's application!

—REBECCA GOTTESMAN,
Assistant Principal, Locust Valley High School

A.

1. Keep their focus—remain academically engaged.

2. Don't develop senioritis.

3. Continue to think about which college community will serve their growth and development.

—NANETTE TARBOUNI,
Director, College Counseling, John Burroughs School

Q. Are there admissions missteps you observe repeatedly that you would like to caution future college applicants about?

A. Families are often very focused on the application process and can forget about deadlines for the financial aid process. Late applications for financial aid are a huge mistake and cost families money in lost scholarships.

We advise our students to complete their essay over the summer before their senior year. It helps to get what is seen as one of the most torturous parts of the application underway before students have the nightly load of homework, athletic practices, and other commitments added. There are always a few who don't take the advice and end up regretting it later.

Submitting supplementary information to colleges, like art portfolios and musical recordings, can be a confusing process. Refer directly to the institutional websites for directions—one size does not fit all! If in doubt, don't guess; call the college directly.

—AMY BAUMGARTEL SINGER,
Director of College Counseling, The Wheeler School

A. Remember that there are 24 hours in a day. If the total daily hours on your list of activities adds up to more than 24, it calls them all into question.

1. Check your spelling!!!

2. Don't forget to send your scores.

3. Don't have your parents make calls that you can make.

4. Apply to a balanced list of schools.

Remember that the most important school on your list is the one you love, you can afford, and that you know you will get into. When I think of the word "safety" I think of seat belts, air bags, and the little yellow oxygen mask that drops out of the ceiling if the plane is going to crash! We are all glad that these things exist, but do you really want to try them out? Same thing applies to the safety school concept. Find a solid backup option you can live with.

—PAUL W. HORGAN,
Director of College Counseling, Cape Henry Collegiate School

A. Parents can be too involved—students need to do their own work, including the typing.

—NANETTE TARBOUNI,
Director, College Counseling, John Burroughs School

Q. We would appreciate any additional comments or anecdotes you would like to share.

A. We have a panel of our seniors come to an annual junior retreat in the spring and talk about their experiences with the process. Everything from managing deadlines, visiting colleges, writing the essays, and managing the expectations of teachers and parents is discussed. When students hear this information from their peers, it is a powerful way for them to get good information.

Communicate with the teachers who are writing your recommendations early. They spend hours of their own time writing these recommendations and a last-minute ask to a teacher is asking for a "last-minute" effort from a busy teacher. Also, be sure to thank your teacher with a handwritten note—respectful communication goes a long way!

Stay organized! No pun intended with the title of the book, but this is the most surefire way to minimize the stress of the college process.

—AMY BAUMGARTEL SINGER,
Director of College Counseling, The Wheeler School

A. The college application process is an ever-changing process! Every year changes occur with respect to application criteria, modifications to the admissions process, and variations of the deadlines.

The college application process is a progression. Start early and break it up into small, manageable tasks. Most important, utilize all the resources available to you!

—REBECCA GOTTESMAN,
Assistant Principal, Locust Valley High School

A. The college application process is far easier than the process of deciding where to send them. Most of the application is personal information, objective data, and relatively simple answers. The essays can be paralyzing to even the brightest students, but ultimately there is a lot of time and support available to get them done.

My advice for getting into college is to *apply to the right schools.* It may sound overly simplistic, but when a college reader sees a student who fits their institution, that student is most likely to get the benefit of the doubt. If you apply to schools where your academic performance is far below their standards, there isn't really anything you can do in your application to make a positive difference. You are getting a thin envelope. When you apply to a place where your academic record is near the top of their pool of applicants, you have to go to great lengths on the application to blow it. Where the rubber hits the road on apps is at the schools where the giant domino is teetering back and forth. Do a good job and it may fall in your favor. Make careless errors and rush through it, and the domino might fall right back on your head. The point: look for the right fit, both academically and personally, and you are likely to have some great options for life after high school.

—PAUL W. HORGAN,
Director of College Counseling, Cape Henry Collegiate School

RESOURCES

TEST REGISTRATION

SAT and SAT Subject Tests
https://collegereadiness.collegeboard.org/sat/register/international

ACT
https://www.act.org/content/act/en/products-and-services/the-act-non-us/registration.html

TOEFL
https://www.ets.org/toefl

IELTS
https://www.ieltsregistration.org/ieltscandidate/candidateonline/home.html

Test Optional
http://fairtest.org/university/optional

TEST PREP

SAT Practice Tests
https://collegereadiness.collegeboard.org/sat/practice/full-length-practice-tests

https://cb.collegeboard.org/sat/better-takes-practice/index.html

College Board Daily Practice App
https://collegereadiness.collegeboard.org/sat/practice/daily-practice-app

SAT Free Sample Practice Questions
https://collegereadiness.collegeboard.org/sample-questions

ACT Test Prep
https://www.act.org/content/act/en/products-and-ser-
vices/the-act-non-us/test-preparation.html

TOEFL Test Prep
https://www.ets.org/toefl/ibt/prepare/

IELTS Test Prep
https://www.ielts.org/en-us/book-a-test/prepare-for-your-ielts-test

FINANCIAL AID

Net Price Calculator
https://collegecost.ed.gov/netpricecenter.aspx

FinAid.org
http://www.finaid.org

Acknowledgments

The idea for our first book, *The College Bound Organizer* was sparked by our own personal experiences with the college admissions process. Our forward thinking team at Mango encouraged us to write *The University Bound Organizer* to address the needs of international students seeking to study in the USA.

We want to thank our agent, Anne Marie O'Farrell, for believing in us. Your experience and guidance set us in the right direction. Your insight paired us with the perfect publisher, Mango Media. Thank you Chris McKenney, your innovative approach to publishing and marketing delivered our book to readers throughout the world. Brenda Knight, your insight and support allowed us to turn our concept into an exciting reality. Elina Diaz, your creative process helped bring our book to life.

Barbara Kelly Vessa, we are indebted to you on so many levels for your unwavering support. You have worn many hats: great friend, wise legal counsel and trusted advisor.

Emmy Liss, once again you so graciously offered to serve as our go-to, on-call editorial and technical support team. Your ingenuity, perceptiveness and endless patience are priceless gifts you shared.

Thank you to the many admissions professionals who generously offered their time and thoughts. We are confident our readers will find your insight invaluable as they navigate the college admissions process in the USA.

Our six university graduates opened the door to the world of higher education admissions, enabling us the take off on a new path. You make us so proud!

George and Sam, thank you for cheering us on!

About the Authors

Anna Costaras and Gail Liss are co-authors of *The University Bound Organizer*. Their goal is to provide international students and their parents with the inside information, insight and resources necessary to meet the demands of applying to college in the United States.

As co-founders of Bound to Organize LLC, their mission is to empower students to successfully navigate the complicated and stressful college application process. "Our efforts are focused on providing guidance and support for all college bound students, regardless of where they apply." Through their website, Bound to Organize and on Facebook, readers are updated with the latest news from the world of higher education and provided with all the resources necessary to get from college search to move-in day.

Anna Costaras holds a BS and MBA from New York University Stern School of Business. She is the founder of a college-bound mentoring program for underserved students and is actively involved in an educational enrichment program for children in need of after-school support, having served as a volunteer, college mentor, and as a member of the board of directors.

Anna is a veteran of the college application process, having guided her three children on their paths to both undergraduate and graduate university programs. She lives in New York with her husband.

Gail Liss earned a MBA from New York University Stern School of Business, studied at The London School of Economics, and holds a BA from the University of Rochester. She is actively involved in a non-profit providing college bound support for inner city students and works with children in teen arts programs.

Gail counseled her three children through the application process, both undergraduate and graduate, and survived to write about it. She lives in New York with her husband.

CPSIA information can be obtained
at www.ICGtesting.com
Printed in the USA
BVHW092305030919
557328BV00002B/2/P